From Eden to Armageddon

FROM EDEN TO ARMAGEDDON

A Biblical History of the World in

Classic Art and Illustration

Selected and Edited by

DENNY L. BROWN

SHADOW MOUNTAIN

Library of Congress Cataloging-in-Publication Data

Bible. English. Authorized. Selections. 1995.
   From Eden to Armageddon / selected and edited by Denny L. Brown.
     p.   cm.
   ISBN 1-57345-371-4 (hardcover)
   1. Bible—Quotations. 2. Bible—History of Biblical events.
  3. Bible—Prophecies—End of the world. I. Brown, Denny L., 1936–   .
  II. Title.
  BS432.B72   1998
  220.9'5—dc21   97-47719
                                                     CIP

Printed in the United States of America   42316-6363

10 9 8 7 6 5 4 3 2 1

Contents

The Present

The Future

PREFACE

This book, as its title suggests, is an attempt to present the biblical chronicles as depicted through art by the great masters. As history has shown, art is the natural vehicle to complement scripture: we never tire of it, and it enables us to contemplate experience at an elevated level of feeling. Great art enriches our understanding. Every time we look at it we discover new aspects and layers of meaning, much as we do reading the poetry of the Bible. Both art and scripture reflect the experience we bring to it. Together art and scripture provide powerful insights—they are the perfect combination to heighten experience.

For centuries scripture was thought to be the only fit subject for artists. Because of that, many paintings for this book could be placed alongside the scriptures that inspired them. Working to bring together the scriptures and the art was an exhilarating process. I looked for scriptural depth in the art, and many first choices were replaced as artists worked their inspiration on me. Although many choices were intensely personal, almost all have universal appeal. More art was included than originally planned because some paintings would not go away: they simply chose themselves. In a few instances works have been used in settings other than those intended by the artists because in some cases no proper art was found to illustrate important biblical events. But great art often transcends its subject to shed light on objects separated in time and distance to become startlingly appropriate.

After selecting the paintings, I found it inspiring to reread the passages that had intrigued the artists, discovering their fervor through the same words that had led them to such awesome, spiritual creativity. It is strangely comforting to know that the biblical passages we read today are the same passages that centuries ago moved these master painters to such divine labors. This commingling of art and spirit leads us to discover over and over again the wisdom, power, and inspiration of those even greater masters who have given us the Bible itself.

Dates have been assigned to the important events throughout history that are depicted in this book. It should be noted that these dates were derived from many different sources on the history of the world. Biblical dates are, of course, open to interpretation; the process of arriving at such dates includes some speculation and at times even sparks contention among scholars and scientists alike. However, these dates provide a broad framework in which to view the pivotal events of biblical history.

Thank you for sharing in these great events of history and biblical destiny. I am confident that every time you take this journey, your experience will be richer and deeper than before.

ACKNOWLEDGMENTS

I would like to thank the many people who helped in the creation of this book. My research was a pleasant experience as I became acquainted with many different people of diverse professions in museums and galleries around the world. We often hear of the decay of polite society, but my experience has proved the opposite. Most people are not only pleasant but genuinely good. Decent people are very much the same worldwide, differing only in custom and language. Imagine my surprise when I requested an image in one of the great museums of the world and was kindly invited to peruse their files at my leisure. This and other privileges transcended the business interest of the museums. To be treated, without exception, with courtesy and kindness in all parts of the world, whether in person, by telephone, or through the mail, has been truly remarkable. The world is yet imbued with kindness.

Thanks also goes to my brother A. C. Brown for his encouragement, his writing, and his many other services; and to my wife, Jeri, for consulting with me and for her many valuable suggestions. Ann Parkinson and Chrissy Clyde were of great help in acquiring transparencies for the artwork.

Jonathan Saltzman deserves special recognition for his many hours in developing the original design and layout for the book. My thanks also goes to Poppy R. Andrew and Melanie D. Seyer for their work with color processing.

I would also like to express appreciation to the publishing staff of Shadow Mountain. Special thanks to Ronald O. Stucki, for his creativity and help with designing the book, Jack M. Lyon and Jennifer Pritchett for their editorial assistance, and Patricia J. Parkinson for her typographical work.

FROM EDEN TO ARMAGEDDON

A Biblical History of the World in Classic Art and Illustration

FROM EDEN TO ARMAGEDDON

THE PAST

CREATION OF THE WORLD

In the beginning
God created the heaven and the earth.

And God said,
Let the waters under the heaven
be gathered together unto one place,
and let the dry land appear:
and it was so.

And God called the dry land Earth;
and the gathering together of the waters
called he Seas:
and God saw that it was good.

These are the generations of the heavens
and of the earth when they were created,
in the day that the Lord God made
the earth and the heavens.

For he spake, and it was done;
he commanded, and it stood fast.

❧ *Genesis 1:1, 9–10; 2:4;*
Psalm 33:9

Michelangelo Buonarroti, *The Creation of the Sun, Moon and Earth* (detail). SISTINE CHAPEL, VATICAN PALACE, VATICAN.

COMPLETED WORLD

HE stretcheth out the north
over the empty place,
and hangeth the earth upon nothing.

He bindeth up the waters in his thick clouds;
and the cloud is not rent under them.

He holdeth back the face of his throne,
and spreadeth his cloud upon it.

He hath compassed the waters with bounds,
until the day and night come to an end.

The pillars of heaven tremble
and are astonished at his reproof.

He divideth the sea with his power,
and by his understanding
he smiteth through the proud.

By his spirit he hath garnished the heavens;
his hand hath formed the crooked serpent.

Lo, these are parts of his ways;
but how little a portion is heard of him?
but the thunder of his power
who can understand?

 *Job 26:7–14*

Raphael, *Separation of the Land from the Water*
(detail). LOGGE, VATICAN PALACE, VATICAN.

War in Heaven

And there was war in heaven: Michael
and his angels fought against the dragon;
and the dragon fought and his angels,

And prevailed not; neither was
their place found any more in heaven.

And the great dragon was cast out,
that old serpent, called the Devil, and Satan,
which deceiveth the whole world:
he was cast out into the earth,
and his angels were cast out with him.

And I heard a loud voice saying in heaven,
Now is come salvation, and strength,
and the kingdom of our God, and the
power of his Christ: for the accuser
of our brethren is cast down, which accused
them before our God day and night.

And they overcame him by the blood of
the Lamb, and by the word of their testimony;
and they loved not their lives unto the death.

Therefore rejoice, ye heavens, and ye that
dwell in them. Woe to the inhabiters
of the earth and of the sea!
for the devil is come down
unto you, having great wrath, because
he knoweth that he hath but a short time.

❧ *Revelation 12:7–12*

Domenico Beccafumi, *Saint Michael Archangel
and the Fall of the Rebel Angels.* PINACOTECA
NAZIONALE, SIENA, ITALY.

GARDEN OF EDEN

AND the Lord God formed man
of the dust of the ground,
and breathed into his nostrils
the breath of life;
and man became a living soul.

And the Lord God planted a garden
eastward in Eden; and there he put
the man whom he had formed.

And out of the ground
made the Lord God to grow
every tree that is pleasant to the sight,
and good for food;
the tree of life also in the midst of the garden,
and the tree of knowledge of good and evil.

And the Lord God took the man,
and put him into the garden of Eden
to dress it and to keep it.

And the Lord God said,
It is not good that the man should be alone;
I will make him an help meet for him.

And the rib,
which the Lord God had taken from man,
made he a woman,
and brought her unto the man.

❧ *Genesis 2:7–9, 15, 18, 22*

Nicolas Poussin, *Spring, or Paradise on Earth.*
LOUVRE, PARIS, FRANCE.

EXPULSION FROM THE GARDEN

AND Adam called his wife's name Eve;
because she was the mother of all living.

Unto Adam also and to his wife
did the Lord God make coats of skins,
and clothed them.

And the Lord God said, Behold,
the man is become as one of us,
to know good and evil: and now,
lest he put forth his hand,
and take also of the tree of life,
and eat, and live for ever:

Therefore the Lord God
sent him forth from the garden
of Eden, to till the ground
from whence he was taken.

So he drove out the man;
and he placed at the east
of the garden of Eden
Cherubims, and a flaming sword
which turned every way,
to keep the way of the tree of life.

ॐ *Genesis 3:20–24*

Thomas Cole, *Expulsion from the Garden of Eden.*
GIFT OF MRS. MAXIM KAROLIK FOR THE M. AND
M. KAROLIK COLLECTION OF AMERICAN PAINTINGS,
1815–1865. COURTESY OF MUSEUM OF FINE ARTS,
BOSTON, MASSACHUSETTS.

CAIN SLAYS ABEL

3880 B.C.

AND . . . it came to pass, that Cain
brought of the fruit of the ground
an offering unto the Lord.

And Abel, he also brought of the firstlings
of his flock and of the fat thereof.
And the Lord had respect unto Abel
and to his offering:

But unto Cain and to his offering
he had not respect.
And Cain was very wroth,
and his countenance fell.

And the Lord said unto Cain, Why art thou wroth?
and why is thy countenance fallen?

If thou doest well, shalt thou not be accepted?
and if thou doest not well, sin lieth at the door.
And unto thee shall be his desire,
and thou shalt rule over him.

And Cain talked with Abel his brother:
and it came to pass, when they were in the field,
that Cain rose up against Abel his brother,
and slew him.

Genesis 4:3–8

Jacopo Robusti Tintoretto, *Cain Slays Abel.*
THE GALLERIE DELL' ACCADEMIA, VENICE, ITALY.

POPULATION OF THE EARTH FROM ADAM TO ENOCH

3950–2350 B.C.

AND Adam . . . begat . . . Seth . . . and he begat sons
and daughters: and all the days that Adam lived
were nine hundred and thirty years.

And Seth . . . begat Enos . . . and begat sons
and daughters: and all the days of Seth were
nine hundred and twelve years.

And Enos . . . begat Cainan . . . and begat sons
and daughters: and all the days of Enos were
nine hundred and five years.

And Cainan . . . begat Mahalaleel . . . and begat
sons and daughters: and all the days of Cainan
were nine hundred and ten years.

And Mahalaleel . . . begat Jared . . . and begat
sons and daughters: and all the days of Mahalaleel
were eight hundred and ninety and five years.

And Jared . . . begat Enoch . . . and begat sons
and daughters: and all the days of Jared were
nine hundred sixty and two years.

❧ *Genesis 5:3–20*

Kadar-Konecsni, *Before the Storm* (detail).
THE HUNGARIAN NATIONAL GALLERY,
BUDAPEST, HUNGARY.

TRANSLATION OF THE PROPHET ENOCH

2950 B.C.

AND Enoch lived sixty and five years,
and begat Methuselah:

And Enoch walked with God
after he begat Methuselah
three hundred years,
and begat sons and daughters:

And all the days of Enoch were
three hundred sixty and five years:

And Enoch walked with God:
and he was not;
for God took him.

By faith Enoch was translated
that he should not see death;
and was not found,
because God had translated him:
for before his translation he had
this testimony, that he pleased God.

❧ *Genesis 5:21–24;*
Hebrews 11:5

Antonio Domenico Gabbiani, *Triumph
of the Corsini Family.* GALLERIA CORSINI,
FLORENCE, ITALY.

Hans Makart, *The Plague in Florence.* GEORG
SCHÄFER COLLECTION, STADTISCHES
MUSEUM, SCHWEINFURT, GERMANY.

CORRUPT WORLD
BEFORE THE FLOOD

2350 B.C.

AND God saw that the wickedness of man was
great in the earth, and that every imagination of
the thoughts of his heart was only evil continually.

The earth also was corrupt before God,
and the earth was filled with violence.

And God looked upon the earth, and,
behold, it was corrupt; for all flesh
had corrupted his way upon the earth.

❧ *Genesis 6:5, 11–12*

NOAH'S ARK

2350 B.C.

Jacopo da Ponte Bassano, *Animals Entering the Ark* (detail). MUSEO NACIONAL DEL PRADO, MADRID, SPAIN.

AND God said unto Noah,
The end of all flesh is come before me;
for the earth is filled with violence
through them; and, behold,
I will destroy them with the earth.

Make thee an ark of gopher wood;
rooms shalt thou make in the ark,
and shalt pitch it within and
without with pitch.

And, behold, I, even I, do bring a flood
of waters upon the earth, to destroy
all flesh, wherein is the breath of life,
from under heaven; and every thing
that is in the earth shall die.

But with thee will I establish my covenant;
and thou shalt come into the ark, thou,
and thy sons, and thy wife, and
thy sons' wives with thee.

And of every living thing of all flesh,
two of every sort shalt thou bring
into the ark, to keep them alive
with thee; they shall be male and female.

Of fowls after their kind, and of cattle
after their kind, of every creeping thing
of the earth.

Thus did Noah; according to all
that God commanded him.

Genesis 6:13–14, 17–20, 22

James Jacques Joseph Tissot, *The Animals Enter the Ark.* JEWISH MUSEUM, NEW YORK.

THE FLOOD

2350 B.C.

And the rain was upon the earth
forty days and forty nights.

And the waters increased, and bare up the ark,
and it was lift up above the earth.

❧ *Genesis 7:12, 17*

Paolo Uccello, *The Deluge*
(detail). S. MARIA NOVELLA,
FLORENCE, ITALY.

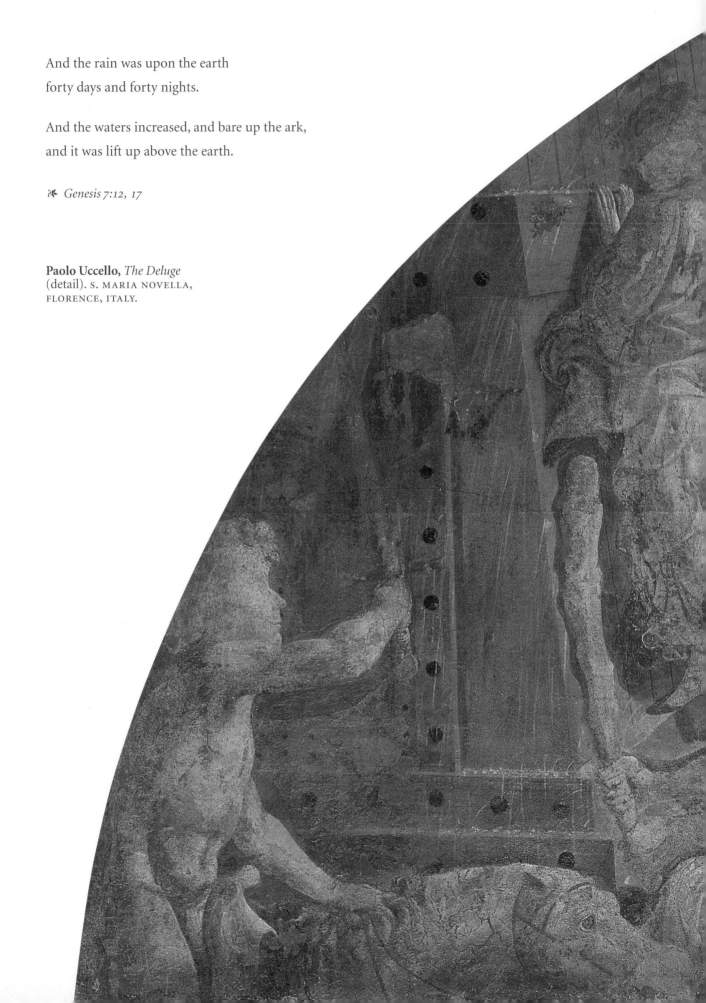

THE WATERS PREVAIL

2350 B.C.

AND the waters prevailed exceedingly
upon the earth; and all the high hills,
that were under the whole heaven,
were covered.

And every living substance
was destroyed which was upon
the face of the ground, both man,
and cattle, and the creeping things,
and the fowl of the heaven;
and they were destroyed
from the earth: and
Noah only remained alive, and
they that were with him in the ark.

❧ *Genesis 7:19, 23*

Nicolas Poussin, *Winter, or The Flood.*
LOUVRE, PARIS, FRANCE.

SUBSIDING OF THE WATERS

2349 B.C.

AND God remembered Noah,
and every living thing,
and all the cattle that was with him in the ark:
and God made a wind to pass over the earth,
and the waters asswaged;

The fountains also of the deep and
the windows of heaven were stopped,
and the rain from heaven was restrained;

And the waters returned
from off the earth continually:
and after the end of the hundred and fifty days
the waters were abated.

And it came to pass at the end of forty days,
that Noah opened the window of the ark
which he had made:

Also he sent forth a dove from him,
to see if the waters were abated
from off the face of the ground;

And the dove came in to him in the evening;
and, lo, in her mouth
was an olive leaf pluckt off:
so Noah knew that the waters were abated
from off the earth.

Genesis 8:1–3, 6, 8, 11

Thomas Cole, *The Subsiding of the Waters of the Deluge.*
NATIONAL MUSEUM OF AMERICAN ART, SMITHSONIAN
INSTITUTE, WASHINGTON, D.C. GIFT OF MRS. KATIE DEAN
IN MEMORY OF MINNIBEL S. AND JAMES WALLACE DEAN
AND MUSEUM PURCHASE THROUGH THE SMITHSONIAN
COLLECTIONS ACQUISITION PROGRAM.

Michelangelo Buonarroti, *The Sacrifice of Noah* (detail).
SISTINE CHAPEL, VATICAN PALACE, VATICAN.

After the Flood

2349 B.C.

And it came to pass
in the six hundredth and first year,
in the first month,
the first day of the month,
the waters were dried up from off the earth:
and Noah removed the covering of the ark,
and looked, and, behold,
the face of the ground was dry.

And Noah went forth,
and his sons, and his wife,
and his sons' wives with him:

Every beast,
every creeping thing,
and every fowl,
and whatsoever creepeth upon the earth,
after their kinds,
went forth out of the ark.

And Noah builded an altar unto the Lord;
and took of every clean beast,
and of every clean fowl,
and offered burnt offerings on the altar.

Genesis 8:13, 18–20

TOWER OF BABEL

2220 B.C.

AND the whole earth was of
one language, and of one speech.

And they said, Go to,
let us build us a city and a tower,
whose top may reach unto heaven;
and let us make us a name,
lest we be scattered abroad
upon the face of the whole earth.

And the Lord came down
to see the city and the tower,
which the children of men builded.

Go to, let us go down,
and there confound their language,
that they may not understand
one another's speech.

Therefore is the name
of it called Babel;
because the Lord did there confound
the language of all the earth:
and from thence
did the Lord scatter them abroad
upon the face of all the earth.

❧ *Genesis 11:1, 4–5, 7, 9*

Pieter Brueghel the Elder, *The Tower of Babel.*
MUSEUM BOYMANS VAN BEUNINGEN, ROTTERDAM,
THE NETHERLANDS.

ABRAHAM IN UR
OF THE CHALDEES

1996 B.C.

ABRAHAM lived in Ur of the Chaldees
in the southern part of Mesopotamia
(the land between the Tigris and
Euphrates rivers), west of the Persian Gulf
in modern-day Iraq.

Ur was part of a people who produced
the first extensive civilization known
to history. At one point Ur had all western
Asia under its sway and proclaimed
the first extensive code of laws in history.

The city grew rich by trade
that flowed through it on the Euphrates
and it was made beautiful with temples.
At one time the city was ruled so wisely
that the people deified the ruler
as a god who had brought back
their ancient Paradise.

Its glory was short and the city was
soon sacked and ruled by Elam
from the East, which in turn was soon
conquered and ruled by Babylon.

❧ *See Will Durant,* Our Oriental Heritage, *122–23*

Michael A. Hampshire. Ur of the Chaldees.
Workaday Ur Prepares for a Festival.
ⒸNATIONAL GEOGRAPHIC SOCIETY.

John M. McDermott. Ur of the Chaldees.
"Stairway for the Gods"—A Ziggurat of Ur.
©NATIONAL GEOGRAPHIC SOCIETY.

ABRAHAM LEAVES
UR OF THE CHALDEES

1996 B.C.

AND Terah lived seventy years,
and begat Abram, Nahor, and Haran.

And Haran died before his father Terah in
the land of his nativity, in Ur of the Chaldees.

And Abram and Nahor took them wives:
the name of Abram's wife was Sarai;

And Terah took Abram his son, and Lot
the son of Haran his son's son, and Sarai
his daughter in law, his son Abram's wife; and
they went forth with them from Ur of the
Chaldees, to go into the land of Canaan;
and they came unto Haran, and dwelt there.

❧ *Genesis 11:26, 28–29, 31*

ABRAHAM ENTERS
THE LAND OF CANAAN*

1921 B.C.

Now the Lord had said unto Abram,
Get thee out of thy country,
and from thy kindred,
and from thy father's house,
unto a land that I will shew thee:

And I will make of thee
a great nation,
and I will bless thee,
and make thy name great;
and thou shalt be a blessing:

And I will bless them that bless thee,
and curse him that curseth thee:
and in thee shall all families of the earth
be blessed.

And Abram took Sarai his wife, and
Lot his brother's son, and all their
substance that they had gathered,
and the souls that they had gotten
in Haran; and they went forth
to go into the land of Canaan; and
into the land of Canaan they came.

ఇ *Genesis 12:1–3, 5*

*Palestine

James Jacques Joseph Tissot, *The Caravan
of Abram.* JEWISH MUSEUM, NEW YORK.

MEETING OF ABRAHAM AND MELCHIZEDEK, KING OF SALEM*

1910 B.C.

AND when Abram heard that his brother
was taken captive, he armed his trained servants, . . .
and pursued them unto Dan.

And he divided himself against them . . . by night,
and smote them, and pursued them unto Hobah,
which is on the left hand of Damascus.

And Melchizedek king of Salem
brought forth bread and wine:
and he was the priest of the most high God.

And he blessed them, and said,
Blessed be Abram of the most high God,
possessor of heaven and earth:

And blessed be the most high God,
which hath delivered thine enemies into thy hand.
And he gave him tithes of all.

Now consider how great this man was,
unto whom even the patriarch Abraham
gave the tenth of the spoils.

꙳ *Genesis 14:14–15, 18–20;
Hebrews 7:4*

*Jerusalem

Peter Paul Rubens, *The Meeting of Abraham
and Melchizedek.* © 1996 BOARD OF TRUSTEES,
NATIONAL GALLERY OF ART, WASHINGTON, D.C.

Three Angels
Appear to Abraham

1895 B.C.

And the Lord appeared unto him
in the plains of Mamre:
and he sat in the tent door in the heat of the day;

And said, My Lord, if now I have found favour in thy
sight, pass not away, I pray thee, from thy servant:

And they said unto him, Where is Sarah thy wife?
And he said, Behold, in the tent.

And he said, I will certainly return unto thee
according to the time of life;
and, lo, Sarah thy wife shall have a son.
And Sarah heard it in the tent door,
which was behind him.

Now Abraham and Sarah were old and well stricken
in age; and it ceased to be with Sarah
after the manner of women.

Therefore Sarah laughed within herself, saying,
After I am waxed old shall I have pleasure,
my lord being old also?

And the Lord said, Shall I hide from Abraham
that thing which I do;

Seeing that Abraham shall surely become
a great and mighty nation, and all the nations
of the earth shall be blessed in him?

❧ *Genesis 18:1, 3, 9–12, 17–18*

Three Angels
Appear to Abraham

[42]

Giovanni Domenico Tiepolo, *The Three Angels Appearing to Abraham.*
THE GALLERIE DELL' ACCADEMIA, VENICE, ITALY.

Jacob (Israel) Meets Rachel

1780 B.C.

THEN Jacob went on his journey,
and came into the land of the people of the east.

And Jacob said unto them, My brethren,
whence be ye? And they said, Of Haran are we.

And he said unto them, Know ye Laban
the son of Nahor? And they said, We know him.

And he said unto them, Is he well?
And they said, He is well: and, behold,
Rachel his daughter cometh with the sheep.

And while he yet spake with them,
Rachel came with her father's sheep:
for she kept them.

And it came to pass, when Jacob saw Rachel
the daughter of Laban his mother's brother,
and the sheep of Laban his mother's brother,
that Jacob went near, and rolled the stone
from the well's mouth, and watered the flock
of Laban his mother's brother.

And Jacob kissed Rachel, and lifted up his voice,
and wept.

ক *Genesis 29:1, 4–6, 9–11*

William Dice, *The Meeting of Jacob and Rachel.*
LEICESTERSHIRE MUSEUMS, LEICESTER, ENGLAND.

EGYPT

2325–560 B.C.

Egypt

2325–560 B.C.

AND there was a famine in the land:
and Abram went down into Egypt
to sojourn there;
for the famine was grievous in the land.

❧ Genesis 12:10

DURING the reign of Amenhotep III
Egypt was brought into the acme of her splendor.

In his reign Thebes was as majestic as any city
in history. Her streets crowded with merchants,
her markets filled with the goods of the world,
her buildings surpassing in magnificence
all those of ancient or modern capitals,
her imposing palaces receiving tribute from
an endless chain of vassal states, her massive
temples enriched all over with gold and
adorned with every art, her spacious villas
and costly chateaux, her shaded promenades
and artificial lakes providing the scene
for sumptuous displays of fashion
that anticipated Imperial Rome—such was
Egypt's capital in the days of her glory.

❧ Will Durant, Our Oriental Heritage, *155*

Opposite: Detail of the back of the throne of
Tutankhamen, 18th dynasty. EGYPTIAN MUSEUM,
CAIRO, EGYPT.

Pages 46–47: **Charles Theodore (Bey),** *Pyramids and Plain
at Giza after the Flooding of the Nile.* WHITFORD & HUGHES,
LONDON, ENGLAND.

JOSEPH IN EGYPT

1720 B.C.

AND Pharaoh said unto Joseph,
Forasmuch as God hath shewed thee all this,
there is none so discreet and wise as thou art:

Thou shalt be over my house, and according
unto thy word shall all my people be ruled:
only in the throne will I be greater than thou.

And Pharaoh said unto Joseph,
See, I have set thee over all the land of Egypt.

And Pharaoh took off his ring from his hand, and
put it upon Joseph's hand, and arrayed him in vestures
of fine linen, and put a gold chain about his neck;

Then Joseph came and told Pharaoh, and said,
My father and my brethren, and their flocks, and their
herds, and all that they have, are come out of the land
of Canaan; and, behold, they are in the land of Goshen.

And he took some of his brethren, even five men,
and presented them unto Pharaoh.

And Pharaoh spake unto Joseph, saying,
Thy father and thy brethren are come unto thee:

The land of Egypt is before thee; in the best
of the land make thy father and brethren to dwell;
in the land of Goshen let them dwell: and
if thou knowest any men of activity among them,
then make them rulers over my cattle.

ૐ *Genesis 41:39–42; 47:1–2, 5–6*

James Jacques Joseph Tissot, *Joseph and His Brethren
Welcomed by Pharaoh.* JEWISH MUSEUM, NEW YORK.

Lawrence Alma-Tadema, *The Finding of Moses.* PRIVATE COLLECTION.
COURTESY OF DR. VERN G. SWANSON, SPRINGVILLE, UTAH.

MOSES

1450 B.C.

AND Pharaoh charged all his people,
saying, Every son that is born
ye shall cast into the river.

And there went a man of the house of Levi,
and took to wife a daughter of Levi.

And the woman conceived, and bare a son:
and when she saw him
that he was a goodly child,
she hid him three months.

And when she could not longer hide him,
she took for him an ark of bulrushes,
and daubed it with slime and with pitch,
and put the child therein; and she laid it
in the flags by the river's brink.

And the daughter of Pharaoh came down
to wash herself at the river; and her maidens
walked along by the river's side;
and when she saw the ark among the flags,
she sent her maid to fetch it.

And he became her son.
And she called his name Moses:
and she said,
Because I drew him out of the water.

Exodus 1:22; 2:1–3, 5, 10

MOSES AND
THE BURNING BUSH

1370 B.C.

NOW Moses kept the flock of Jethro
his father in law, the priest of Midian:
. . . and came to the mountain of God,
even to Horeb.

And the angel of the Lord
appeared unto him in a flame
of fire out of the midst of a bush:
and he looked, and, behold, . . .
the bush was not consumed.

And when the Lord saw
that he turned aside to see,
God called unto him
out of the midst of the bush,
and said, Moses, Moses.
And he said, Here am I.

And he said, Draw not nigh hither:
put off thy shoes from off thy feet,
for the place whereon thou standest
is holy ground.

And the Lord said,
I have surely seen the affliction
of my people which are in Egypt,
and have heard their cry
by reason of their taskmasters;
for I know their sorrows.

Come now therefore, and I will send thee
unto Pharaoh, that thou mayest
bring forth my people
the children of Israel out of Egypt.

 Exodus 3:1–2, 4–5, 7, 10

Domenico Fetti, *Moses and the Burning Bush.* KUNSTHISTORISCHES MUSEUM, VIENNA, AUSTRIA.

ISRAEL'S EXODUS FROM EGYPT

1370 B.C.

AND it came to pass,
that at midnight the Lord smote
all the firstborn in the land of Egypt,
from the firstborn of Pharaoh
that sat on his throne
unto the firstborn of the captive
that was in the dungeon;
and all the firstborn of cattle.

And he called for Moses and Aaron
by night, and said, Rise up,
and get you forth from among my people,
both ye and the children of Israel;
and go, serve the Lord, as ye have said.

And the people took their dough
before it was leavened,
their kneadingtroughs being bound up
in their clothes upon their shoulders.

And the children of Israel journeyed
from Rameses to Succoth,
about six hundred thousand on foot
that were men, beside children.

❧ *Exodus 12:29, 31, 34, 37*

David Roberts, *The Departure of the Israelites.*
BIRMINGHAM MUSEUMS & ART GALLERY,
BIRMINGHAM, ENGLAND.

Manna in the Wilderness

1370–1330 B.C.

Then said the Lord unto Moses, Behold,
I will rain bread from heaven for you;
and the people shall go out and gather
a certain rate every day.

And when the dew that lay was gone up,
behold, upon the face of the wilderness
there lay a small round thing,
as small as the hoar frost on the ground.

And when the children of Israel saw it,
they said one to another, It is manna:
for they wist not what it was.
And Moses said unto them, This is the bread
which the Lord hath given you to eat.

And they gathered it every morning,
every man according to his eating:
and when the sun waxed hot, it melted.

And the children of Israel did eat manna
forty years, until they came to a land inhabited;
they did eat manna, until they came
unto the borders of the land of Canaan.

❧ *Exodus 16:4, 14–15, 21, 35*

Nicolas Poussin, *The Israelites Gathering Manna
in the Desert.* LOUVRE, PARIS, FRANCE.

MOSES AND THE BRAZEN SERPENT

1370–1330 B.C.

AND the Lord sent fiery serpents
among the people,
and they bit the people;
and much people of Israel died.

Therefore the people came to Moses,
and said, We have sinned, for we have spoken
against the Lord, and against thee;
pray unto the Lord,
that he take away the serpents from us.
And Moses prayed for the people.

And the Lord said unto Moses,
Make thee a fiery serpent,
and set it upon a pole:
and it shall come to pass,
that every one that is bitten,
when he looketh upon it,
shall live.

And Moses made a serpent of brass,
and put it upon a pole,
and it came to pass,
that if a serpent had bitten any man,
when he beheld the serpent of brass,
he lived.

❧ *Numbers 21:6–9*

Anthony van Dyck, *Moses and the Brazen Serpent.*
MUSEO NACIONAL DEL PRADO, MADRID, SPAIN.

Assyria Invades Egypt

650 B.C.

THE burden of Egypt. Behold,
the Lord rideth upon a swift cloud,
and shall come into Egypt:
and the idols of Egypt shall be moved
at his presence, and the heart of Egypt
shall melt in the midst of it.

And the Egyptians will I give over
into the hand of a cruel lord;
and a fierce king shall rule over them,
saith the Lord, the Lord of hosts.

So shall the king of Assyria
lead away the Egyptians prisoners,
and the Ethiopians captives,
young and old, naked and barefoot,
even with their buttocks uncovered,
to the shame of Egypt.

And the inhabitant of this isle
shall say in that day,
Behold, such is our expectation,
whither we flee for help
to be delivered from the king of Assyria:
and how shall we escape?

ex *Isaiah 19:1, 4; 20:4, 6*

H. M. Herget, *Queen Amun-dyek-het of Egypt Is Questioned by Her Captor, King Esarhaddon of Assyria.* © NATIONAL GEOGRAPHIC SOCIETY.

BABYLON
INVADES EGYPT
560 B.C.

THUS saith the Lord God;
I will also make the multitude
of Egypt to cease by the hand of
Nebuchadrezzar king of Babylon.

He and his people with him,
the terrible of the nations,
shall be brought to destroy
the land: and they shall draw
their swords against Egypt,
and fill the land with the slain.

And I will make the rivers dry,
and sell the land into the hand of
the wicked: and I will make the
land waste, and all that is therein,
by the hand of strangers:
I the Lord have spoken it.

And I will strengthen the arms
of the king of Babylon,
and put my sword in his hand:
but I will break Pharaoh's arms,
and he shall groan before him
with the groanings
of a deadly wounded man.

Ezekiel 30:10–12, 24

John Martin, *Pandemonium.*
FORBES MAGAZINE COLLECTION,
NEW YORK CITY, NEW YORK.

David Roberts, *The Island of Philae, Nubia.*
FINE ART SOCIETY, LONDON, ENGLAND.

DESOLATE EGYPT

560 B.C.

THEREFORE thus saith the Lord God;
Behold, I will bring a sword upon thee,
and cut off man and beast out of thee.

And the land of Egypt shall be desolate and
waste; and they shall know that I am the Lord:
because he hath said, The river is mine,
and I have made it.

Behold, therefore I am against thee,
and against thy rivers, and I will make

the land of Egypt utterly waste and
desolate, from the tower of Syene
even unto the border of Ethiopia.

✣ *Ezekiel 29:8–10*

ASSYRIA

1300–612 B.C.

RISE OF ASSYRIA

1300–612 B.C.

BEHOLD, the Assyrian was a cedar
in Lebanon with fair branches, and with
a shadowing shroud, and of an high stature;
and his top was among the thick boughs.

Therefore his height was exalted above
all the trees of the field, and his boughs
were multiplied, and his branches became
long because of the multitude of waters,
when he shot forth.

Thus was he fair in his greatness,
in the length of his branches:
for his root was by great waters.

The cedars in the garden of God
could not hide him: the fir trees
were not like his boughs, and the
chestnut trees were not like his branches;
nor any tree in the garden of God
was like unto him in his beauty.

I have made him fair
by the multitude of his branches:
so that all the trees of Eden, that were in
the garden of God, envied him.

୬ *Ezekiel 31:3, 5, 7–9*

The Prophet Ezekiel

Michelangelo Buonarroti.
THE SISTINE CHAPEL,
VATICAN PALACE, VATICAN.

Opposite: Assyria (detail).
BETTMANN ARCHIVES, NEW YORK.

Pages 68–69: **James Ferguson,** *Nimrud* (detail).
RODNEY G. SEABRIGHT COLLECTION, VICTORIA
ALBERT MUSEUM, LONDON, ENGLAND.

RULE OF ASSYRIA*

1300–612 B.C.

FOR, lo, I raise up the Chaldeans,

that bitter and hasty nation,

which shall march through the breadth

of the land, to possess the dwelling places

that are not theirs.

They are terrible and dreadful:

their judgment and their dignity

shall proceed of themselves.

Their horses also are swifter than

the leopards, and are more fierce than

the evening wolves: and their horsemen

shall spread themselves, and their

horsemen shall come from far; they shall

fly as the eagle that hasteth to eat.

They shall come all for violence:

their faces shall sup up as the east wind,

and they shall gather the captivity

as the sand.

And they shall scoff at the kings, and

the princes shall be a scorn unto them:

they shall deride every strong hold;

for they shall heap dust, and take it.

⁂ *Habakkuk 1:6–10*

*In ancient Mesopotamia, the fertile land between the Tigris and Euphrates rivers in what is now Iraq, the Assyrian empire grew around its principal cities, Asbur and Nineveh. The army ruled, spending its energies in wars of destruction, plunder, and conquest. Even by the standards of the time, the Assyrian warriors were especially hardened in battle, cruelly torturing captives and ruling by terror. They often scattered the people of conquered states to various parts of the empire to prevent revolts. Assyria became the most extensive civilization yet seen in the Mediterranean world, ruling over Sumeria, Babylonia, Elam, Armenia, Syria, Palestine, and Egypt.

Austin Henry Layard, *Hall in Assyrian Temple* (detail).
RODNEY G. SEABRIGHT COLLECTION, VICTORIA
ALBERT MUSEUM, LONDON, ENGLAND.

THE PROPHET ELIJAH VISITED BY AN ANGEL

860 B.C.

AND Elijah said unto them, Take the prophets
of Baal; let not one of them escape.
And they took them: and Elijah brought them
down to the brook Kishon, and slew them there.

And Ahab told Jezebel all that Elijah had done,
and withal how he had slain all the prophets
with the sword.

Then Jezebel sent a messenger unto Elijah,
saying, So let the gods do to me, and more also,
if I make not thy life as the life of one of them
by to morrow about this time.

And when he saw that, he arose, and went
for his life, and came to Beer-sheba, which
belongeth to Judah, and left his servant there.

And as he lay and slept under a juniper tree,
behold, then an angel touched him,
and said unto him, Arise and eat.

And he looked, and, behold, there was a cake
baken on the coals, and a cruse of water
at his head. And he did eat and drink.

And the angel of the Lord came again the second
time, and touched him, and said, Arise and
eat; because the journey is too great for thee.

❧ *1 Kings 18:40; 19:1–3, 5–7*

Peter Paul Rubens, *The Prophet Elijah Receives*
Bread and Water from an Angel (detail).
MUSEE BONNAT, BAYONNE, FRANCE.

JONAH PREACHES TO THE ASSYRIANS IN NINEVEH

775 B.C.

AND the word of the Lord
came unto Jonah the second time,
saying,

Arise, go unto Nineveh, that great city,
and preach unto it
the preaching that I bid thee.

So Jonah arose, and went unto Nineveh,
according to the word of the Lord.
Now Nineveh was an exceeding great city
of three days' journey.

And Jonah began to enter
into the city a day's journey,
and he cried, and said, Yet forty days,
and Nineveh shall be overthrown.

So the people of Nineveh believed God,
and proclaimed a fast,
and put on sackcloth, from the greatest
of them even to the least of them.

And God saw their works,
that they turned from their evil way;
and God repented of the evil,
that he had said that he would do
unto them; and he did it not.

Jonah 3:1–5, 10

Gustave Doré, *Jonah Preaching to the Ninevites.*
THE DORÉ BIBLE.

The Prophet Jonah

Michelangelo Buonarroti.
THE SISTINE CHAPEL,
VATICAN PALACE, VATICAN.

King Shalmaneser of Assyria Takes Captive Samaria*

721 B.C.

The Lost Ten Tribes are to return to the land of their inheritance, Samaria, in the last days (see pages 218–21).

THEN the king of Assyria came up throughout
all the land, and went up to Samaria,
and besieged it three years.

In the ninth year of Hoshea the king of Assyria
took Samaria, and carried Israel away into Assyria,
and placed them in Halah and in Habor by
the river of Gozan, and in the cities of the Medes.

Samaria shall become desolate; for she hath rebelled
against her God: they shall fall by the sword:
their infants shall be dashed in pieces,
and their women with child shall be ripped up.

Therefore I will make Samaria as an heap of
the field, and as plantings of a vineyard: and
I will pour down the stones thereof into the valley,
and I will discover the foundations thereof.

*2 Kings 17:5–6;
Hosea 13:16; Micah 1:6*

Opposite: **G. D. Rowlandson,** *Prisoner Is Being Taken.*
BETTMANN ARCHIVES, NEW YORK.

Below: Black stele of Shalmaneser III. *Jehu, King of Israel, Prostrating Himself before King Shalmaneser III of Assyria.*
BRITISH MUSEUM, LONDON, ENGLAND.

SENNACHERIB, KING OF ASSYRIA, BESIEGES JERUSALEM

701 B.C.

Now it came to pass
in the fourteenth year of king Hezekiah,
that Sennacherib king of Assyria
came up against all the defenced cities of Judah,
and took them.

Therefore thus saith the Lord concerning the
king of Assyria, He shall not come into this city,
nor shoot an arrow there, nor come before it
with shields, nor cast a bank against it.

By the way that he came, by the same
shall he return, and shall not come
into this city, saith the Lord.

For I will defend this city to save it for mine
own sake, and for my servant David's sake.

Then the angel of the Lord went forth,
and smote in the camp of the Assyrians
a hundred and fourscore and five thousand:
and when they arose early in the morning,
behold, they were all dead corpses.

So Sennacherib king of Assyria departed,
and went and returned, and dwelt at Nineveh.

Isaiah 36:1; 37:33–37

Peter Paul Rubens, *Sennacherib before Jerusalem.* ALTE
PINAKOTHEK MUSEUM, MUNICH, GERMANY.

FALL OF NINEVEH

612 B.C.

BUT Nineveh is of old like a pool of water:
yet they shall flee away.
Stand, stand, shall they cry;
but none shall look back.

Woe to the bloody city!
it is all full of lies and robbery;
the prey departeth not;

The noise of a whip,
and the noise of the rattling of the wheels,
and of the pransing horses,
and of the jumping chariots.

Because of the multitude of the
whoredoms of the wellfavoured harlot,
the mistress of witchcrafts,
that selleth nations through her whoredoms,
and families through her witchcrafts.

And it shall come to pass,
that all they that look upon thee
shall flee from thee, and say,
Nineveh is laid waste: who will bemoan her?
whence shall I seek comforters for thee?

❧ *Nahum 2:8; 3:1–2, 4, 7*

John Martin, *The Fall of Nineveh* (detail).
VICTORIA & ALBERT MUSEUM, LONDON,
ENGLAND.

DESOLATE ASSYRIA

612 B.C.

AND he will stretch out his hand
against the north, and destroy Assyria;
and will make Nineveh a desolation,
and dry like a wilderness.

And flocks shall lie down
in the midst of her,
all the beasts of the nations:
both the cormorant and the bittern
shall lodge in the upper lintels
of it; their voice shall sing
in the windows; desolation shall be
in the thresholds: for he shall
uncover the cedar work.

This is the rejoicing city that dwelt
carelessly, that said in her heart,
I am, and there is none beside me:
how is she become a desolation,
a place for beasts to lie down in!
every one that passeth by her
shall hiss, and wag his hand.

☙ *Zephaniah 2:13–15*

Austin Henry Layard, *Watercolor of Nineveh.*
RODNEY G. SEABRIGHT COLLECTION,
VICTORIA & ALBERT MUSEUM, LONDON,
ENGLAND.

BABYLONIA

600–535 B.C.

BABYLON *

600–535 B.C.

O thou king, the most high God
gave Nebuchadnezzar thy father a kingdom,
and majesty, and glory, and honour:

And for the majesty that he gave him,
all people, nations, and languages, trembled
and feared before him: whom he would he slew;
and whom he would he kept alive;
and whom he would he set up;
and whom he would he put down.

And wheresoever the children of men dwell,
the beasts of the field and the fowls of the heaven
hath he given into thine hand,
and hath made thee ruler over them all.

All this came upon the king Nebuchadnezzar.

At the end of twelve months
he walked in the palace of the kingdom of Babylon.

The king spake, and said,
Is not this great Babylon, that I have built
for the house of the kingdom
by the might of my power,
and for the honour of my majesty?

❧ *Daniel 5:18–19; 2:38; 4:28–30*

*In the fertile land between the Tigris and Euphrates rivers, Babylonia repeated the success of Assyria. Babylon, its capital, was the largest and most magnificent city in the world. Its walls, the great temple of Baal, and the hanging gardens were the wonder of the ancient world. The Babylonians made great advances in science, architecture, physics, mathematics, philosophy, language, and medicine. At the height of its power, Babylonia defeated Egypt and Palestine and controlled the Persian Gulf to the Mediterranean Sea. "Babylon" is used in the Bible to denote "the great evil" when referring to Rome or to the great antagonist of the Messiah's kingdom.

Opposite: **H. M. Herget.** *A Babylonian Procession Greets the New Year (during the reign of Nebuchadnezzar).* © NATIONAL GEOGRAPHIC SOCIETY.

Pages 86–87: After a drawing by **Joseph Bogg Beale,** *Wall and Hanging Gardens of Babylon.* BETTMANN ARCHIVES, NEW YORK.

David Blossom, *Painting of Babylon.*
©NATIONAL GEOGRAPHIC SOCIETY.

HANGING GARDENS
OF BABYLON

600–535 B.C.

SUPPORTED on a succession of superimposed
circular colonnades, were the famous Hanging
Gardens, which the Greeks included among
the Seven Wonders of the World.

The gallant Nebuchadnezzar had built them for one of his wives. . . . This princess, unaccustomed to the hot sun and dust of Babylon, pined for the verdure of her native hills. The topmost terrace was covered with rich soil to the depth of many feet, providing space and nourishment not merely for varied flowers and plants, but for the largest and most deep-rooted trees. . . . Here, seventy-five feet above the ground, in the cool shade of tall trees, and surrounded by exotic shrubs and fragrant flowers, the ladies of the royal harem walked unveiled.

❧ *Will Durant*, Our Oriental Heritage, *225*

THE PROPHET DANIEL INTERPRETS KING NEBUCHADNEZZAR'S DREAM *

597 B.C.

The Prophet Daniel

Michelangelo Buonarroti.
THE SISTINE CHAPEL,
VATICAN PALACE, VATICAN.

**King Nebuchadnezzar's
dream is fulfilled as interpreted by the prophet
Daniel (on pages 107,
121, 137, 204–9, 224).*

THOU, O king, sawest, and behold a great image.
This great image, whose brightness was excellent,
stood before thee; and the form thereof was terrible.

This image's head was of fine gold,
his breast and his arms of silver,
his belly and his thighs of brass,

His legs of iron,
his feet part of iron and part of clay.

Thou sawest till that a stone was cut out
without hands, which smote the image
upon his feet that were of iron and clay,
and brake them to pieces.

Then was the iron, the clay, the brass, the silver, and
the gold, broken to pieces together, and became like
the chaff of the summer threshingfloors; and the wind
carried them away, that no place was found for them:
and the stone that smote the image became
a great mountain, and filled the whole earth.

Thou, O king, art a king of kings:
for the God of heaven hath given thee a kingdom,
power, and strength, and glory.

Thou art this head of gold.

≈ Daniel 2:31–35, 37–38

Stuart Paul Heimdal, *Nebuchadnezzar's Giant.*
PRIVATE COLLECTION.

JERUSALEM TAKEN CAPTIVE BY KING NEBUCHADNEZZAR

586 B.C.

AND it came to pass in the ninth year
of his reign . . . that Nebuchadnezzar
king of Babylon came, he, and all his host,
against Jerusalem, and pitched against it;
and they built forts against it round about.

And the city was besieged
unto the eleventh year of king Zedekiah.

And on the ninth day of the fourth month
the famine prevailed in the city, and there
was no bread for the people of the land.

And the city was broken up,
and all the men of war fled by night.

And they burnt the house of God,
and brake down the wall of Jerusalem,
and burnt all the palaces thereof with fire,
and destroyed all the goodly vessels thereof.

And them that had escaped from the sword
carried he away to Babylon.

❧ *2 Kings 25:1–4;
2 Chronicles 36:19–20*

James Jacques Joseph Tissot, *The Flight of
the Prisoners.* JEWISH MUSEUM, NEW YORK.

CAPTIVITY OF JUDAH IN BABYLON

586 B.C.

By the rivers of Babylon, there we sat down,
yea, we wept, when we remembered Zion.

We hanged our harps upon the willows
in the midst thereof.

For there they that carried us away captive
required of us a song; and they that wasted us
required of us mirth, saying,
Sing us one of the songs of Zion.

How shall we sing the Lord's song
in a strange land?

If I forget thee, O Jerusalem,

let my right hand forget her cunning.

If I do not remember thee,

let my tongue cleave to the roof of my mouth;

if I prefer not Jerusalem above my chief joy.

Psalm 137:1–6

Eduard von Bendemann,
The Sorrowing Jews in Exile.
WALLRAF-RICHARTZ MUSEUMS,
COLOGNE, GERMANY.

BELSHAZZAR'S FEAST

535 B.C.

THEN was Daniel brought in
before the king. And the king spake
and said unto Daniel,

I have heard of thee, that thou canst
make interpretations, and dissolve doubts.

Then Daniel answered
and said before the king,

O thou king, the most high God gave
Nebuchadnezzar thy father a kingdom,
and majesty, and glory, and honour:

And for the majesty that he gave him,
all people, nations, and languages,
trembled and feared before him:
whom he would he slew;
and whom he would he kept alive;
and whom he would he set up;
and whom he would he put down.

And thou his son, O Belshazzar,
hast not humbled thine heart,
though thou knewest all this.

In that night was Belshazzar
the king of the Chaldeans slain.

Daniel 5:13, 16–19, 22, 30

Rembrandt Harmensz van Rijn,
Belshazzar's Feast. NATIONAL GALLERY,
LONDON, ENGLAND.

Thomas Cole, *The Course of Empire: Destruction.*
COLLECTION OF THE NEW-YORK HISTORICAL
SOCIETY, NEW YORK.

DESTRUCTION OF
BABYLON BY CYRUS
OF PERSIA

535 B.C.

FOR, lo, I will raise and cause to come
up against Babylon an assembly of great
nations from the north country: and they
shall set themselves in array against her;

They shall hold the bow and the lance:
they are cruel, and will not shew mercy:

their voice shall roar like the sea,
and they shall ride upon horses,
every one put in array, like a man
to the battle, against thee,
O daughter of Babylon.

ॐ *Jeremiah 50:9, 42*

[101]

Thomas Cole, *The Course of Empire: Desolation.*
COLLECTION OF THE NEW-YORK HISTORICAL
SOCIETY, NEW YORK.

DESOLATE BABYLON

535 B.C.

And Babylon shall become heaps, a dwellingplace
for dragons, an astonishment, and an hissing,
without an inhabitant.

Then shalt thou say,
O Lord, thou hast spoken against this place,
to cut it off, that none shall remain in it,
neither man nor beast,
but that it shall be desolate for ever.

And it shall be no more inhabited for ever;
neither shall it be dwelt in

from generation to generation.

As God overthrew Sodom and Gomorrah
and the neighbour cities thereof, saith the Lord;
so shall no man abide there,
neither shall any son of man dwell therein.

❧ *Jeremiah 51:37, 62; 50:39–40*

[103]

PERSIAN
EMPIRE

539–331 B.C.

King Cyrus of Persia

539 B.C.

AND after thee shall arise another kingdom
inferior to thee [Babylon] . . .

This image's . . . breast and his arms of silver . . .

❧ *Daniel 2:39, 32*

THUS saith the Lord to his anointed, to Cyrus,
whose right hand I have holden, to subdue nations
before him; and I will loose the loins of kings,
to open before him the two leaved gates;
and the gates shall not be shut;

I will go before thee, and make the crooked places
straight: I will break in pieces the gates of brass,
and cut in sunder the bars of iron:

And I will give thee the treasures of darkness,
and hidden riches of secret places, that thou mayest
know that I, the Lord, which call thee by thy name,
am the God of Israel.

I have raised him [Cyrus] up in righteousness,
and I will direct all his ways: he shall build my city,
and he shall let go my captives, not for price
nor reward, saith the Lord of hosts.

❧ *Isaiah 45:1–3, 13*

*Continued fulfillment of
Nebuchadnezzar's dream
as interpreted by Daniel
(see page 92).*

Opposite: **Gustave Doré,** *Cyrus Restoring the Vessels of the
Temple.* THE DORÉ BIBLE.

Pages 104–5: **John Martin,** *The Triumph of Mordecai.*
COURTESY OF MR. & MRS. CHRISTIAN B. PEPER, SAINT
LOUIS, MISSOURI.

ESTHER AND KING AHASUERUS

475 B.C.

Now in Shushan the palace there was
a certain Jew, whose name was Mordecai . . .

Who had been carried away from Jerusalem
with the captivity which had been
carried away with Jeconiah king of Judah,
whom Nebuchadnezzar the king of Babylon
had carried away.

And he brought up Hadassah, that is, Esther,
his uncle's daughter: for she had neither father
nor mother, and the maid was fair and beautiful;
whom Mordecai, when her father and mother
were dead, took for his own daughter.

And the king loved Esther above all
the women, and she obtained grace and favour
in his sight more than all the virgins;
so that he set the royal crown upon her head,
and made her queen instead of Vashti.

Then the king made a great feast unto all his
princes and his servants, even Esther's feast;
and he made a release to the provinces,
and gave gifts, according to the state of the king.

Esther 2:5–7, 17–18

Peter Paul Rubens, *Esther before Ahasuerus.*
GERMALDEGALERIE DER BILDENDEN KUNSTE,
VIENNA, AUSTRIA.

MORDECAI'S TRIUMPHANT RIDE THROUGH SUSA, CAPITAL OF PERSIA

475 B.C.

AND Haman answered the king, For the man
whom the king delighteth to honour,

Let the royal apparel be brought
which the king useth to wear, and the horse
that the king rideth upon, and the crown
royal which is set upon his head:

And let this apparel and horse be delivered
to the hand of one of the king's most noble
princes, that they may array the man withal
whom the king delighteth to honour, and
bring him on horseback through the street
of the city, and proclaim before him.

Then the king said to Haman, Make haste,
and take the apparel and the horse,
as thou hast said, and do even so to
Mordecai the Jew, that sitteth at the king's gate:
let nothing fail of all that thou hast spoken.

For Mordecai the Jew was next unto king
Ahasuerus, and great among the Jews,
and accepted of the multitude of his brethren,
seeking the wealth of his people,
and speaking peace to all his seed.

ᵚ *Esther 6:7–10; 10:3*

Paolo Veronese, *Triumph of Mordecai.*
ST. SEBASTIANO, VENICE, ITALY.

King Artaxerxes of Persia Grants Liberty to Judah *

450 B.C.

*Persia was founded on the hot, dry, mountainous area north of the Persian Gulf in what is now part of Iran. It established capital cities at Susa, Ecbatana, and Persepolis, and rapidly expanded, eventually conquering more territory than any nation before in history. At the height of its empire it ruled from India to Egypt, from the Caucasus Mountains to the Arabian Sea, encompassing Afghanistan, Armenia, Cappadocia, Assyria, Babylonia, Syria, Palestine, and Egypt.

The Persians, a handsome and tolerant people, established an empire of self-governing states allowing freedom of religion and allowing captives to return to their homelands. Thus the Jews, held by the Babylonians, were free to return to Jerusalem.

Artaxerxes, king of kings,
unto Ezra the priest, a scribe of the law
of the God of heaven, perfect peace,
and at such a time.

I make a decree, that all they
of the people of Israel,
and of his priests and Levites,
in my realm, which are minded
of their own freewill
to go up to Jerusalem, go with thee.

And I, even I Artaxerxes the king,
do make a decree to all the treasurers
which are beyond the river, that
whatsoever Ezra the priest, the scribe
of the law of the God of heaven,
shall require of you, it be done speedily.

And whosoever will not do the law
of thy God, and the law of the king,
let judgment be executed speedily
upon him, whether it be unto death,
or to banishment, or to confiscation
of goods, or to imprisonment.

❧ *Ezra 7:12–13, 21, 26*

Gustave Doré, *Artaxerxes Granting Liberty to the Jews.*
THE DORÉ BIBLE.

Tom Lovell, *Alexander Burning Persepolis.*
© NATIONAL GEOGRAPHIC SOCIETY.

ALEXANDER THE GREAT DESTROYS PERSEPOLIS, CAPITAL OF PERSIA

331 B.C.

AND as I was considering,
behold, an he goat [Greece] came
from the west on the face
of the whole earth, and touched not
the ground: and the goat had
a notable horn between his eyes.

And he came to the ram [Persia]
that had two horns, which I had seen
standing before the river, and ran
unto him in the fury of his power.

And I saw him come close
unto the ram, and he was moved
with choler against him,
and smote the ram,
and brake his two horns:
and there was no power
in the ram to stand before him,
but he cast him down to the ground,
and stamped upon him:
and there was none that could
deliver the ram out of his hand.

❧ *Daniel 8:5–7*

Frank and Helen Schreider, *Ruins of Persepolis.*
© NATIONAL GEOGRAPHIC SOCIETY.

DESOLATE PERSIA

330 B.C.

THE ram which thou sawest having two
horns are the kings of Media and Persia.

And the rough goat is the king of Grecia:
and the great horn that is between his eyes
is the first king.

Then said he, Knowest thou wherefore
I come unto thee?
and now will I return to fight
with the prince of Persia:
and when I am gone forth,
lo, the prince of Grecia shall come.

Daniel 8:20–21; 10:20

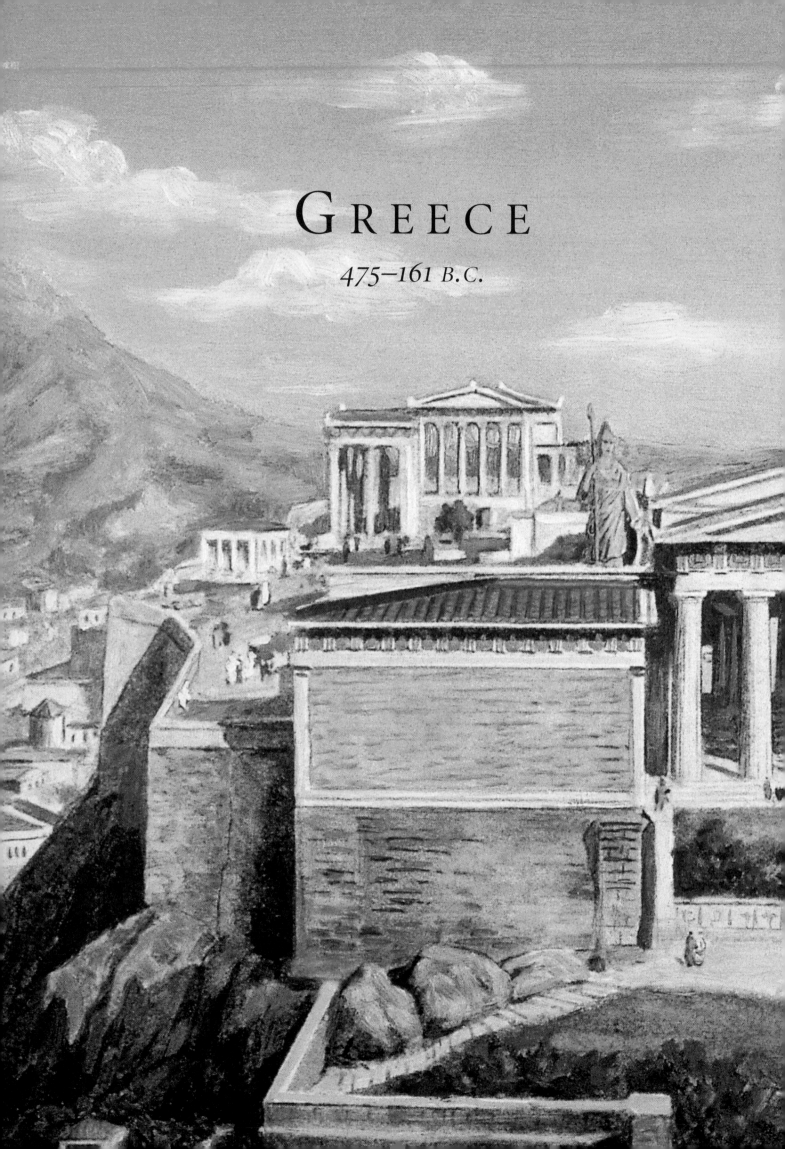

GREECE

475–161 B.C.

RISE OF GREECE

475–161 B.C.

AND after thee [Babylon] shall arise . . .
another third kingdom of brass,
which shall bear rule over all the earth.

This image's . . . belly and his thighs of brass.

⁊ Daniel 2:39, 32

WHEN I have bent Judah for me,
filled the bow with Ephraim,
and raised up thy sons, O Zion,
against thy sons, O Greece,
and made thee as the sword of a mighty man.

⁊ Zechariah 9:13

*Continued fulfillment of
Nebuchadnezzar's dream
as interpreted by Daniel
(see page 92).*

AND when he had gone over those parts,
and had given them much exhortation,
he came into Greece.

And it came to pass in Iconium, that they went
both together into the synagogue of the Jews,
and so spake, that a great multitude both
of the Jews and also of the Greeks believed.

⁊ Acts 20:2; 14:1

Opposite: **Raphael,** *The School of Athens: Plato and Aristotle*
(detail). STANZA DELLA SEGNATURA, VATICAN PALACE,
VATICAN.

Pages 118–19: After reconstruction by **Tpeisch,**
The Acropolis, Athens. BETTMANN ARCHIVES, NEW YORK.

GREECE

475–161 B.C.

EXCEPTING machinery, there is hardly
anything secular in our culture that does not
come from Greece. Schools, gymnasiums,
arithmetic, geometry, history, rhetoric,
physics, biology, anatomy, hygiene, therapy,
cosmetics, poetry, music, tragedy, comedy,
philosophy, theology, agnosticism, skepticism,
stoicism, epicureanism, ethics, politics,
idealism, philanthropy, cynicism, tyranny,
plutocracy, democracy: these are all Greek
words for cultural forms seldom originated,
but in many cases first matured for good or
evil by the abounding energy of the Greeks.

All the problems that disturb us today—
the cutting down of forests and the erosion
of the soil; . . . the limitation of the family; . . .
the corruptions of politics and the perversions
of conduct; the conflict of religion and science; . . .
the war of the classes; . . . the struggle between
democracy and dictatorship, . . . between the East
and the West—all these agitated, as if for our
instruction, the brilliant and turbulent life
of ancient Hellas. There is nothing in Greek
civilization that does not illuminate our own.

⯮ *Will Durant,* The Life of Greece, *vii–viii*

Raphael, *School of Athens* (detail).
STANZA DELLA SEGNATURA, VATICAN
PALACE, VATICAN.

ALEXANDER
OCCUPIES BABYLON

331 B.C.

IN the wake of Alexander's
generals, we see Greek civilization,
too powerful for its little peninsula,
burst its narrow bounds, and
overflow into Asia, Africa, and Italy;
teaching the cult of the body and
the intellect to the mystical Orient,
reviving the glories of Egypt in
Ptolemaic Alexandria, and enriching
Rhodes with trade and art;
developing geometry with Euclid
at Alexandria and Archimedes
at Syracuse; formulating in Zeno
and Epicurus the most lasting
philosophies in history; carving the
Aphrodite of Melos, the *Laocoön,*
the *Victory of Samothrace,* and the
Altar of Pergamum.

Alexander received the submission
of Babylon, partook of its wealth,
distributed some of it to his soldiers,
but charmed the city by making
obeisance to its gods, and decreeing
the restoration of its sacred shrines.

❧ *See Will Durant,* The Life of Greece, *viii, 545*

Charles Le Brun, *Alexander the Great Enters Babylon.* LOUVRE, PARIS, FRANCE.

ALEXANDER MARRIES THE DAUGHTERS OF THE KINGS OF PERSIA

324 B.C.

MORE and more charmed by his new subjects, he abandoned the idea of ruling over them as a Macedonian, and conceived himself as a Greco-Persian emperor governing a realm in which Persians and Greeks would be on an equal footing, and would peaceably mingle their culture and their blood. The long quarrel of Europe and Asia would end in a wedding feast.

He broached the plan to his officers, and suggested that they, too, should take Persian wives. They smiled at his hopes of uniting the two nations, but they had been a long time away from home, and the Persian ladies were beautiful. So in one great nuptial at Susa, Alexander married Statira, daughter of Darius III, and Parysatis, daughter of Artaxerxes III, attaching himself in this way to both branches of Persian royalty, while eighty of his officers took Persian brides.

❦ *Will Durant,* The Life of Greece, *547–48*

Tom Lovell. *Marriage of Alexander.* © NATIONAL GEOGRAPHIC SOCIETY.

ALEXANDER IN INDIA

320 B.C.

HE passed over the Himalayas into India. Vanity conspired with curiosity to lead him into such distant territory; his generals advised against it, his army obeyed him unwillingly. Crossing the Indus, he defeated King Porus, and announced that he would continue to the Ganges. But his soldiers refused to go farther. He pled with them, and for three days, like a scion of Achilles, pouted in his tent; but they had had enough. Sadly he turned back, loath to face west again, and forced his way through hostile tribes with such personal bravery that his soldiers wept at their inability to realize all his dreams. He was the first to scale the walls of the Mallians; after he and two others had leaped into the city the ladders broke, and they found themselves alone amidst the enemy. Alexander fought until he sank exhausted by his wounds.

After three months of convalescence he renewed his march along the Indus, and at last reached the Indian Ocean. Alexander himself led . . . his army northwest along the coast of India and through the desert of Gedrosia (Baluchistan), where the sufferings of his men rivaled those of Napoleon's army on the return from Moscow. Heat killed thousands, thirst killed more. A little water was found, and was brought to Alexander, but he deliberately poured it out upon the ground. When the remnants of his force reached Susa some ten thousand had died, and Alexander was half insane.

&❧ *Will Durant*, The Life of Greece, 546–47

Tom Lovell, *Alexander Splashes on to Asian Soil* (detail). © NATIONAL GEOGRAPHIC SOCIETY.

Tom Lovell, *Alexander and the Indian Army* (detail). © NATIONAL GEOGRAPHIC SOCIETY.

FALL OF GREECE
TO ROME

146 B.C.

IN 146 B.C. the League of Cities
of Greece voted for a war
of liberation against Rome.
A fever of patriotism
swept the cities of the League.
Slaves were freed and armed.

The angry Roman Senate sent over
an army and a fleet. Their combined
forces overcame all resistance,
and captured Corinth. The rich
city of merchants and courtesans
was put to the flames,
all the men were slaughtered,
and all the women and children
were sold into slavery.
Whatever wealth could be moved
was carried off to Italy.

All the leaders were put to death.
Greece and Macedonia were united
into one province under a Roman
governor. Boeotia, Locris, Corinth,
and Euboea were subjected to
annual tribute. The turbulent cities
had at last found peace.

❧ *See Will Durant,* The Life of Greece,
665–66

Tony Robert-Fleury, *Le Dernier Jour de Corinthe.* MUSÉE D'ORSAY, PARIS, FRANCE.

Defeated Greece

A.D. 325

CIVILIZATION does not die, it migrates; it changes its habitat and its dress, but it lives on. The decay of one civilization, as of one individual, makes room for the growth of another; life sheds the old skin, and surprises death with fresh youth. Greek civilization is alive; it moves in every breath of mind that we breathe; so much of it remains that none of us in one lifetime could absorb it all.

We know its defects . . . but we will not linger over these blemishes. We will hear behind the turmoil of political history the voices of Solon and Socrates, of Plato and Euripides, of Pheidias and Praxiteles, of Epicurus and Archimedes; we will be grateful for the existence of such men, and will seek their company across alien centuries.

See Will Durant, The Life of Greece, *670–71*

Frederic Edwin Church, *The Parthenon.* BEQUEST OF MARIA DEWITT JESUP,
FROM THE COLLECTION OF HER HUSBAND, MORRIS K. JESUP, 1914. (15.30.67).
PHOTOGRAPH © 1986 THE METROPOLITAN MUSEUM OF ART, NEW YORK.

ROMAN EMPIRE

161 B.C.—A.D. 395

ROMAN EMPIRE

161 B.C.–A.D. 395

AND the fourth kingdom shall be strong as iron:
forasmuch as iron breaketh in pieces and subdueth
all things: and as iron that breaketh all these,
shall it break in pieces and bruise.

This image's . . . legs of iron . . .

❧ *Daniel 2:40, 32–33*

AND Jesus answering said unto them,
Render to Caesar the things that are Caesar's,
and to God the things that are God's.

❧ *Mark 12:17*

*Continued fulfillment of
Nebuchadnezzar's dream
as interpreted by Daniel
(see page 92).*

BUT Paul said unto them,
They have beaten us openly uncondemned,
being Romans, and have cast us into prison;
and now do they thrust us out privily? nay verily;
but let them come themselves and fetch us out.

And the serjeants told these words
unto the magistrates: and they feared,
when they heard that they were Romans.

❧ *Acts 16:37–38*

Opposite: **Lawrence Alma-Tadema,** *The Coliseum.*
PRIVATE COLLECTION.

Pages 134–35: **Joseph Mallord William Turner,**
*Ancient Rome: Agrippina Landing with the Ashes of
Germanicus.* TATE GALLERY, LONDON, ENGLAND.

Bernard D'Andrea. *Emperor Claudius in a Triumphal Procession through the Forum Romanum.* © NATIONAL GEOGRAPHIC SOCIETY.

RISE OF THE ROMAN EMPIRE

161 B.C.–A.D. 395

THE rise of Rome from a crossroads town to world mastery, its achievement of two centuries of security and peace from the Crimea to Gibraltar and from the Euphrates to Hadrian's

Wall, its spread of classic civilization over the Mediterranean and western European world, its struggle to preserve its ordered realm from a surrounding sea of barbarism, its long, slow crumbling and final catastrophic collapse into darkness and chaos—this is surely the greatest drama ever played by man; unless it be that other drama which began when Caesar and Christ stood face to face in Pilate's court, and continued until a handful of hunted Christians had grown by time and patience, and through persecution and terror, to be first the allies, then the masters, and at last the heirs, of the greatest empire in history.

❧ *Will Durant,* Caesar and Christ, *vii*

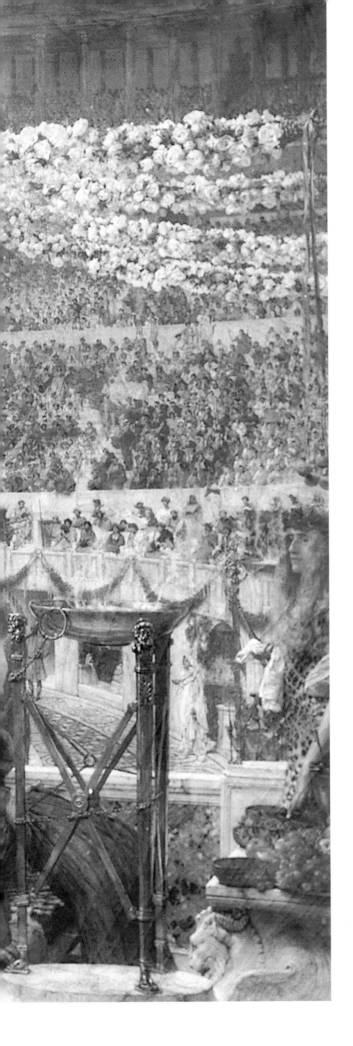

ROMAN EMPIRE IN ITS GLORY

161 B.C.–A.D. 395

THE Empire of Rome comprehended
the fairest part of the earth, and
the most civilized portion of mankind.
The frontiers of that extensive
monarchy were guarded by ancient
renown and disciplined valour.
The gentle but powerful influence
of laws and manners had gradually
cemented the union of the provinces.
Their peaceful inhabitants enjoyed
and abused the advantages of wealth
and luxury.

The Roman name was revered
among the most remote nations
of the earth. The terror of the Roman
arms added weight and dignity
to the moderation of the emperors.
They preserved peace by a constant
preparation for war; and while
justice regulated their conduct, they
announced to the nations on their
confines that they were as little disposed
to endure as to offer an injury.

◌ *Edward Gibbon,* The Decline and Fall of
the Roman Empire, *1, 9*

Lawrence Alma-Tadema, *Caracalla
and Geta.* PRIVATE COLLECTION. COURTESY OF
DR. VERN G. SWANSON, SPRINGVILLE, UTAH.

The Conception
of Christ

1 B.C.

And in the sixth month the angel Gabriel was sent
from God unto a city of Galilee, named Nazareth,

To a virgin espoused to a man whose name
was Joseph, of the house of David;
and the virgin's name was Mary.

And the angel said unto her, Fear not, Mary:
for thou hast found favour with God.

And, behold, thou shalt conceive in thy womb,
and bring forth a son,
and shalt call his name JESUS.

He shall be great, and shall be called
the Son of the Highest:
and the Lord God shall give unto him
the throne of his father David:

And he shall reign over the house of Jacob for ever;
and of his kingdom there shall be no end.

Then said Mary unto the angel, How shall this be,
seeing I know not a man?

And the angel answered and said unto her,
The Holy Ghost shall come upon thee,
and the power of the Highest shall overshadow thee:
therefore also that holy thing which shall be
born of thee shall be called the Son of God.

ℜ *Luke 1:26–27, 30–35*

Giovanni Battista Tiepolo, *The Immaculate
Conception.* MUSEO NACIONAL DEL PRADO, MADRID,
SPAIN.

Annunciation to
the Shepherds

A.D. 1

AND there were in the same country
shepherds abiding in the field,
keeping watch over their flock by night.

And, lo, the angel of the Lord came upon them,
and the glory of the Lord shone round about them:
and they were sore afraid.

And the angel said unto them,
Fear not: for, behold,
I bring you good tidings of great joy,
which shall be to all people.

For unto you is born this day in the city of David
a Saviour, which is Christ the Lord.

And this shall be a sign unto you;
Ye shall find the babe wrapped in swaddling clothes,
lying in a manger.

And suddenly there was with the angel
a multitude of the heavenly host praising God,
and saying,

Glory to God in the highest, and on earth
peace, good will toward men.

⁊ *Luke 2:8–14*

Carl Bloch, *The Shepherds and the Angels.* FREDERIKSBORG
MUSEUM, DENMARK.

BIRTH OF JESUS CHRIST

A.D. 1

THEREFORE the Lord himself
shall give you a sign; Behold,
a virgin shall conceive, and bear a son,
and shall call his name Immanuel.

And he shall be for a sanctuary;
but for a stone of stumbling
and for a rock of offence
to both the houses of Israel,
for a gin and for a snare
to the inhabitants of Jerusalem.

For unto us a child is born,
unto us a son is given: and the
government shall be upon his shoulder:
and his name shall be called
Wonderful, Counsellor,
The mighty God, The everlasting Father,
The Prince of Peace.

Of the increase of his government and
peace there shall be no end, upon
the throne of David, and upon his kingdom,
to order it, and to establish it with judgment
and with justice from henceforth even for ever.
The zeal of the Lord of hosts will perform this.

❦ *Isaiah 7:14; 8:14; 9:6–7*

The Prophet Isaiah

Michelangelo Buonarroti.
THE SISTINE CHAPEL,
VATICAN PALACE, VATICAN.

Rembrandt Harmensz van Rijn, *Adoration of
the Shepherds.* NATIONAL GALLERY, LONDON,
ENGLAND.

FLIGHT INTO EGYPT

A.D. 1–30

THE angel of the Lord
appeareth to Joseph in a dream, saying,
Arise, and take the young child and his mother,
and flee into Egypt, and be thou there
until I bring thee word:

for Herod will seek the young child
to destroy him.

When he arose, he took the young child
and his mother by night,
and departed into Egypt:

And was there until the death of Herod: that it might
be fulfilled which was spoken of the Lord by the prophet,
saying, Out of Egypt have I called my son.

ᚱ *Matthew 2:13–15*

Annibale Carracci, *Flight into Egypt.*
GALLERIA DORIA PAMPHILJ, ROME, ITALY.

Jesus and Joseph in the Carpenter Shop

A.D. 1–30

But when Herod was dead,
behold, an angel of the Lord appeareth
in a dream to Joseph in Egypt.

Saying, Arise, and take, the young child
and his mother, and go into the land of Israel:
for they are dead which sought
the young child's life.

And he arose, and took the young child and
his mother, and came into the land of Israel.

And he came and dwelt in a city called Nazareth:
that it might be fulfilled which was spoken
by the prophets, He shall be called a Nazarene.

And the child grew, and waxed strong
in spirit, filled with wisdom:
and the grace of God was upon him.

❧ *Matthew 2:19–21, 23; Luke 2:40*

Georges de La Tour, *St. Joseph the Carpenter.*
LOUVRE, PARIS, FRANCE.

CHRIST AMONG
THE DOCTORS

A.D. 1–30

Now his parents went to Jerusalem
every year at the feast of the passover.

And when he was twelve years old,
they went up to Jerusalem
after the custom of the feast.

And when they had fulfilled the days,
as they returned, the child Jesus
tarried behind in Jerusalem;
and Joseph and his mother knew not of it.

And it came to pass, that after three days
they found him in the temple,
sitting in the midst of the doctors,
both hearing them, and asking them questions.

And all that heard him were astonished
at his understanding and answers.

And when they saw him, they were amazed:
and his mother said unto him, Son,
why hast thou thus dealt with us? behold,
thy father and I have sought thee sorrowing.

And he said unto them, How is it
that ye sought me? wist ye not that
I must be about my Father's business?

Luke 2:41–43, 46–49

Jusepe de Ribera, *Christ among the Doctors.*
KUNSTHISTORISCHES MUSEUM, VIENNA, AUSTRIA.

Bartolomé Esteban Murillo, *The Marriage Feast at Cana.*
THE BARBER INSTITUTE OF FINE ARTS, BIRMINGHAM, ENGLAND.

MARRIAGE FEAST AT CANA

A.D. 30–33

AND the third day there was a marriage
in Cana of Galilee;
and the mother of Jesus was there:

And when they wanted wine,
the mother of Jesus saith unto him,
They have no wine.

His mother saith unto the servants,
Whatsoever he saith unto you, do it.

And there were set there six waterpots of stone,
after the manner of the purifying of the Jews,
containing two or three firkins apiece.

Jesus saith unto them, Fill the waterpots
with water. And they filled them up to the brim.

And he saith unto them, Draw out now,
and bear unto the governor of the feast.
And they bare it.

When the ruler of the feast had tasted the water
that was made wine, and knew not whence it was:
. . . the governor of the feast called the bridegroom,

And saith unto him, Every man at the beginning
doth set forth good wine; and when men
have well drunk, then that which is worse:
but thou hast kept the good wine until now.

John 2:1, 3, 5–10

CALLING OF MATTHEW

A.D. 30–33

AND after these things he went forth,
and saw a publican, named Levi,*
sitting at the receipt of custom:
and he said unto him, Follow me.

And he left all, rose up,
and followed him.

And Levi made him a great feast
in his own house: and there was
a great company of publicans and
of others that sat down with them.

But their scribes and Pharisees
murmured against his disciples,
saying, Why do ye eat and drink
with publicans and sinners?

And Jesus answering said unto them,
They that are whole need not
a physician; but they that are sick.

I came not to call the righteous,
but sinners to repentance.

❧ *Luke 5:27–32*

*After his conversion, Levi was called Matthew.

Michelangelo Merisi da Caravaggio,
The Calling of Saint Matthew. S. LUIGI DEI
FRANCESI, ROME, ITALY.

Carl Bloch, *The Healing at the Pool of Bethesda.* BETHESDA CHAPEL, COPENHAGEN, DENMARK.

THE HEALING AT THE POOL OF BETHESDA

A.D. 30–33

Now there is at Jerusalem
by the sheep market a pool,
which is called in the Hebrew tongue
Bethesda, having five porches.

In these lay a great multitude
of impotent folk, of blind, halt, withered,
waiting for the moving of the water.

For an angel went down at a certain season
into the pool, and troubled the water:
whosoever then first after the troubling
of the water stepped in was made whole
of whatsoever disease he had.

And a certain man was there, which had
an infirmity thirty and eight years.

When Jesus saw him lie, and knew that
he had been now a long time in that case,
he saith unto him, Wilt thou be made whole?

The impotent man answered him, Sir,
I have no man, when the water is troubled,
to put me into the pool: but while I am
coming, another steppeth down before me.

Jesus saith unto him,
Rise, take up thy bed, and walk.

And immediately the man was made
whole, and took up his bed, and walked:
and on the same day was the sabbath.

❧ *John 5:2–9*

CHRIST CLEARING THE TEMPLE

A.D. 30–33

FOR the zeal of thine house
hath eaten me up; and the
reproaches of them that reproached
thee are fallen upon me.

Psalm 69:9

And the Jews' passover was at hand,
and Jesus went up to Jerusalem,

And found in the temple those
that sold oxen and sheep and doves,
and the changers of money sitting:

And when he had made a scourge
of small cords, he drove them
all out of the temple, and
the sheep, and the oxen; and
poured out the changers' money,
and overthrew the tables;

And said unto them that sold doves,
Take these things hence;
make not my Father's house
an house of merchandise.

And his disciples remembered
that it was written,
The zeal of thine house
hath eaten me up.

John 2:13–17

Giovanni Benedetto Castiglione, *Christ Chasing
the Merchants from the Temple.* LOUVRE,
PARIS, FRANCE.

Leonardo da Vinci, *Last Supper.* S. MARIA DELLE GRAZIE, MILAN, ITALY.

LAST SUPPER

A.D. 33

Now the first day of the feast
of unleavened bread the disciples
came to Jesus, saying unto him,
Where wilt thou that we prepare
for thee to eat the passover?

And he said, Go into the city to such a man,
and say unto him, The Master saith,
My time is at hand; I will keep the passover
at thy house with my disciples.

And the disciples did as Jesus had appointed
them; and they made ready the passover.

Now when the even was come,
he sat down with the twelve.

And as they did eat, he said,
Verily I say unto you,
that one of you shall betray me.

And they were exceeding sorrowful,
and began every one of them
to say unto him, Lord, is it I?

☙ *Matthew 26:17–22*

THE BETRAYAL
OF CHRIST

A.D. 33

RISE up, let us go;
lo, he that betrayeth me is at hand.

And immediately, while he yet spake,
cometh Judas, one of the twelve,
and with him a great multitude with swords and staves,
from the chief priests and the scribes and the elders.

And he that betrayed him had given them a token,
saying, Whomsoever I shall kiss,
that same is he; take him,
and lead him away safely.

And as soon as he was come,
he goeth straightway to him, and saith,
Master, master; and kissed him.

And they laid their hands on him, and took him.

And Jesus answered and said unto them,
Are ye come out, as against a thief,
with swords and with staves to take me?

I was daily with you in the temple teaching,
and ye took me not:
but the scriptures must be fulfilled.

And they all forsook him, and fled.

ᚶ *Mark 14:42–46, 48–50*

Anthony van Dyck, *The Betrayal of Christ.* BRISTOL
MUSEUM & ART GALLERY, BRISTOL, ENGLAND.

THE CRUCIFIXION

A.D. 33

HE is despised and rejected of men;
a man of sorrows, and acquainted with grief:
and we hid as it were our faces from him;
he was despised, and we esteemed him not.

Surely he hath borne our griefs, and carried
our sorrows: yet we did esteem him stricken,
smitten of God, and afflicted.

But he was wounded for our transgressions,
he was bruised for our iniquities:
the chastisement of our peace was upon him;
and with his stripes we are healed.

All we like sheep have gone astray;
we have turned every one to his own way;
and the Lord hath laid on him
the iniquity of us all.

He was oppressed, and he was afflicted,
yet he opened not his mouth:
he is brought as a lamb to the slaughter,
and as a sheep before her shearers is dumb,
so he openeth not his mouth.

He was taken from prison and from judgment:
and who shall declare his generation?
for he was cut off out of the land of the living:
for the transgression of my people was he stricken.

⁂ *Isaiah 53:3–8*

Paolo Veronese, *Calvary.* LOUVRE, PARIS, FRANCE.

DESCENT FROM THE CROSS

A.D. 33

AND he made his grave with the wicked,
and with the rich in his death;
because he had done no violence,
neither was any deceit in his mouth.

Yet it pleased the Lord to bruise him;
he hath put him to grief:
when thou shalt make his soul
an offering for sin, he shall see his seed,
he shall prolong his days, and the pleasure
of the Lord shall prosper in his hand.

He shall see of the travail of his soul,
and shall be satisfied: by his knowledge
shall my righteous servant justify many;
for he shall bear their iniquities.

Therefore will I divide him a portion
with the great, and he shall divide the spoil
with the strong; because he hath poured out
his soul unto death: and he was numbered
with the transgressors; and he bare
the sin of many, and made intercession
for the transgressors.

❧ *Isaiah 53:9–12*

Workshop of **Rembrandt Harmensz van Rijn,**
probably **Constantijn van Renesse,**
The Descent from the Cross. NATIONAL GALLERY
OF ART, WASHINGTON, D.C.

THE ENTOMBMENT

A.D. 33

AND many women were there
beholding afar off, which followed
Jesus from Galilee, ministering unto him:

Among which was Mary Magdalene,
and Mary the mother of James and Joses,
and the mother of Zebedee's children.

When the even was come, there came
a rich man of Arimathæa, named Joseph,
who also himself was Jesus' disciple:

He went to Pilate, and begged
the body of Jesus. Then Pilate
commanded the body to be delivered.

And when Joseph had taken the body,
he wrapped it in a clean linen cloth,

And laid it in his own new tomb,
which he had hewn out in the rock:
and he rolled a great stone to the door
of the sepulchre, and departed.

And there was Mary Magdalene,
and the other Mary,
sitting over against the sepulchre.

⁂ *Matthew 27:55–61*

Tiziano Vecellio [Titian], *The Entombment
of Christ.* MUSEO NACIONAL DEL PRADO,
MADRID, SPAIN.

Hieronymus Bosch, *Paradise* (detail). PALAZZO DUCALE, VENICE, ITALY.

Paradise—Departed
Obedient Spirits Awaiting
the Resurrection

A.D. 33

AND one of the malefactors which were hanged
railed on him, saying,
If thou be Christ, save thyself and us.

But the other answering rebuked him,
saying, Dost not thou fear God,
seeing thou art in the same condemnation?

And we indeed justly; for we receive
the due reward of our deeds:
but this man hath done nothing amiss.

And he said unto Jesus,
Lord, remember me
when thou comest into thy kingdom.

And Jesus said unto him, Verily I say unto thee,
To day shalt thou be with me in paradise.

Luke 23:39–43

Corrado Giacinto, *Paradise.* MUSEO NAZIONALE DI CAPODIMONTE, NAPLES, ITALY.

Spirit Prison—
Departed Disobedient
Spirits Awaiting the
Resurrection

A.D. 33

To give knowledge of salvation unto his people
by the remission of their sins,

Through the tender mercy of our God;
whereby the dayspring from on high hath visited us,

To give light to them that sit in darkness
and in the shadow of death,
to guide our feet into the way of peace.

For Christ also hath once suffered for sins,
the just for the unjust, that he might bring us
to God, being put to death in the flesh,
but quickened by the Spirit:

By which also he went and preached
unto the spirits in prison;

Which sometime were disobedient, when once
the longsuffering of God waited in the days of Noah,
while the ark was a preparing, wherein few,
that is, eight souls were saved by water.

For as Jonas was three days and three nights
in the whale's belly; so shall the Son of man be
three days and three nights in the heart of the earth.

*Luke 1:77–79; 1 Peter 3:18–20;
Matthew 12:40*

Domenico Beccafumi, *Christ in Limbo.* PINACOTECA
NAZIONALE, SIENA, ITALY.

THE RESURRECTION OF CHRIST

A.D. 33

AND, behold, there was a great
earthquake: for the angel of the Lord
descended from heaven, and came
and rolled back the stone
from the door, and sat upon it.

His countenance was like lightning,
and his raiment white as snow:

And for fear of him the keepers
did shake, and became as dead men.

And the angel answered and said
unto the women, Fear not ye:
for I know that ye seek Jesus,
which was crucified.

He is not here: for he is risen,
as he said. Come, see the place
where the Lord lay.

And go quickly, and tell his disciples
that he is risen from the dead;
and, behold, he goeth before you
into Galilee; there shall ye see him:
lo, I have told you.

❧ *Matthew 28:2–7*

Johann Carl Loth, *Resurrection of Christ.*
GALLERIA DEGLI UFFIZI, FLORENCE, ITALY.

Supper at Emmaus

A.D. 33

And, behold, two of them went that same
day to a village called Emmaus, which was
from Jerusalem about threescore furlongs.

And it came to pass, that,
while they communed together and reasoned,
Jesus himself drew near, and went with them.

But their eyes were holden
that they should not know him.

And it came to pass,
as he sat at meat with them,
he took bread, and blessed it,
and brake, and gave to them.

And their eyes were opened,
and they knew him;
and he vanished out of their sight.

And they said one to another,
Did not our heart burn within us,
while he talked with us by the way,
and while he opened to us the scriptures?

⁂ *Luke 24:13, 15–16, 30–32*

Michelangelo Merisi da Caravaggio, *Supper at
Emmaus.* PINACOTECA DI BRERA, MILAN, ITALY.

Giovanni Francesco Barbieri [Il Guercino], *The Incredulity of St. Thomas.* PINACOTECA, VATICAN MUSEUMS, VATICAN.

DOUBTING THOMAS

A.D. 33

BUT Thomas, one of the twelve, called Didymus,
was not with them when Jesus came.

The other disciples therefore said unto him,
We have seen the Lord. But he said unto them,
Except I shall see in his hands the print of the nails,
and put my finger into the print of the nails,
and thrust my hand into his side, I will not believe.

And after eight days again his disciples were within,
and Thomas with them: then came Jesus,
the doors being shut, and stood in the midst,
and said, Peace be unto you.

Then saith he to Thomas,
Reach hither thy finger, and behold my hands;
and reach hither thy hand, and thrust it into my side:
and be not faithless, but believing.

And Thomas answered and said unto him,
My Lord and my God.

Jesus saith unto him, Thomas,
because thou hast seen me, thou hast believed:
blessed are they that have not seen,
and yet have believed.

John 20:24–29

JESUS AND THE APOSTLES AT THE SEA OF TIBERIAS

A.D. 33

AFTER these things Jesus
shewed himself again to the
disciples at the sea of Tiberias;
and on this wise shewed he himself.

Simon Peter saith unto them,
I go a fishing. They say unto him,
We also go with thee.
They went forth, and entered
into a ship immediately; and
that night they caught nothing.

But when the morning was
now come, Jesus stood on the shore:
but the disciples knew not
that it was Jesus.

And he said unto them,
Cast the net on the right side of the ship,
and ye shall find. They cast therefore,
and now they were not able to draw
it for the multitude of fishes.

This is now the third time
that Jesus shewed himself to his disciples,
after that he was risen from the dead.

John 21:1, 3–4, 6, 14

Raphael, *The Miraculous Draught of Fishes.*
VICTORIA & ALBERT MUSEUM, LONDON,
ENGLAND.

[183]

Apostles John, Peter, Paul, and Mark

A.D. 33–70

THEN said Jesus unto them, Be not afraid:
go tell my brethren that they go into Galilee,
and there shall they see me.

Then the eleven disciples went away into Galilee,
into a mountain where Jesus had appointed them.

And when they saw him, they worshipped him:
but some doubted.

And Jesus came and spake unto them, saying,
All power is given unto me in heaven and in earth.

Go ye therefore, and teach all nations,
baptizing them in the name of the Father,
and of the Son, and of the Holy Ghost:

Teaching them to observe all things whatsoever
I have commanded you: and, lo, I am with you
alway, even unto the end of the world. Amen.

⚘ *Matthew 28:10, 16–20*

Opposite: **Albrecht Dürer,** *The Four Apostles.*
ALTE PINAKOTHEK MUSEUM, MUNICH, GERMANY.

Below: **Raphael,** *Saint Paul Preaching in Athens* (detail).
VICTORIA & ALBERT MUSEUM, LONDON, ENGLAND.

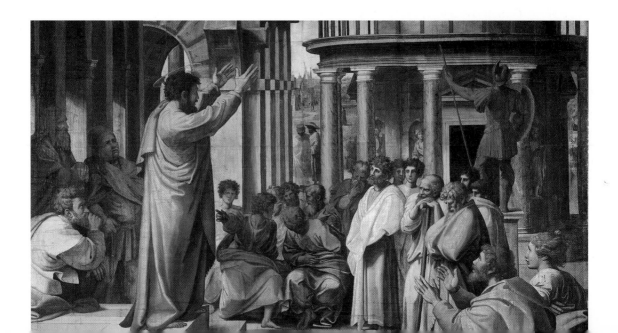

ASCENSION

A.D. 33

AND he said unto them,
These are the words which I spake
unto you, while I was yet with you,
that all things must be fulfilled,
which were written in the law of Moses,
and in the prophets, and in the psalms,
concerning me.

And said unto them, Thus it is written,
and thus it behoved Christ to suffer,
and to rise from the dead the third day:

And that repentance and remission
of sins should be preached in his name
among all nations, beginning at Jerusalem.

And ye are witnesses of these things.

And he led them out as far as to Bethany,
and he lifted up his hands, and blessed them.

And it came to pass,
while he blessed them,
he was parted from them,
and carried up into heaven.

    Luke 24:44, 46–48, 50–51

Rembrandt Harmensz van Rijn,
Ascension. ALTE PINAKOTHEK MUSEUM,
MUNICH, GERMANY.

ROMAN DESTRUCTION OF JERUSALEM BY TITUS

A.D. 70

AND as they led him away, they laid
hold upon one Simon, a Cyrenian,
coming out of the country,
and on him they laid the cross,
that he might bear it after Jesus.

And there followed him
a great company of people,
and of women, which also
bewailed and lamented him.

But Jesus turning unto them
said, Daughters of Jerusalem,
weep not for me, but weep for
yourselves, and for your children.

For, behold, the days are coming,
in the which they shall say,
Blessed are the barren,
and the wombs that never bare,
and the paps which never gave suck.

Then shall they begin to say
to the mountains, Fall on us;
and to the hills, Cover us.

❧ *Luke 23:26–30*

Nicolas Poussin, *Titus in Front of
the Destroyed Temple of Jerusalem.*
KUNSTHISTORISCHES MUSEUM,
VIENNA, AUSTRIA.

RETURN OF TITUS TO ROME

A.D. 71

O GOD, the heathen are come into thine
inheritance; thy holy temple have they defiled;
they have laid Jerusalem on heaps.

The dead bodies of thy servants
have they given to be meat unto
the fowls of the heaven, the flesh of
thy saints unto the beasts of the earth.

Their blood have they shed
like water round about Jerusalem;
and there was none to bury them.

We are become a reproach to
our neighbours, a scorn and derision
to them that are round about us.

Pour out thy wrath upon the heathen that
have not known thee, and upon the kingdoms
that have not called upon thy name.

For they have devoured Jacob,
and laid waste his dwelling place.

❧ Psalm 79:1–4, 6–7

Opposite: **Lawrence Alma-Tadema,** *The Triumph of Titus.*
THE WALTERS ART GALLERY, BALTIMORE, MARYLAND.

Below: Romans with the Spoils from Jerusalem. RELIEF
FROM THE ARCH OF TITUS, ROME, ITALY.

David Roberts, *Tabarias from the Walls, Saffet in the Distance.*
LEICESTERSHIRE MUSEUMS, LEICESTER, ENGLAND.

DESOLATE PALESTINE

A.D. 71

RISE up, ye women that are at ease;
hear my voice, ye careless daughters;
give ear unto my speech.

Many days and years shall ye be troubled,
ye careless women: for the vintage shall fail,
the gathering shall not come.

Tremble, ye women that are at ease;
be troubled, ye careless ones:
strip you, and make you bare,
and gird sackcloth upon your loins.

They shall lament for the teats,
for the pleasant fields, for the fruitful vine.

Upon the land of my people
shall come up thorns and briers;
yea, upon all the houses of joy in the joyous city:

Because the palaces shall be forsaken;
the multitude of the city shall be left;
the forts and towers shall be for dens for ever,
a joy of wild asses, a pasture of flocks;

Until the spirit be poured upon us from on high,
and the wilderness be a fruitful field,
and the fruitful field be counted for a forest.

Isaiah 32:9–15

Peter Paul Rubens, *Death of Decius Mus.*
COLLECTION OF THE GOVERNING PRINCE OF
LIECHTENSTEIN.

DEATH OF EMPEROR DECIUS

A.D. 251

AN obscure town called Forum Terebronii,
was the scene of the battle. . . . The barbarians were
enured to encounters in the bog, their persons tall,

their spears long, such as could wound at a distance.
In the morass the Roman army, after an ineffectual
struggle, was irrecoverably lost; nor could the body
of the emperor ever be found. Such was the fate of
Decius, in the fiftieth year of his age.

⁊ *See Edward Gibbon,* The Decline and Fall of the Roman
Empire, *269*

DECAY OF ROME

A.D. 455

THE opulent nobles of an immense capital, who were never excited by the pursuit of military glory, and seldom engaged in the occupations of civil government, naturally resigned their leisure to the business and amusements of private life. The greater part of the nobles, who dissipated their fortunes in profuse luxury, found themselves poor in the midst of wealth, and idle in a constant round of dissipation.

But this native splendour is degraded and sullied by the conduct of some nobles, who, unmindful of their own dignity and of that of their country, assume an unbounded licence of vice and folly.

But when the prodigal commons had imprudently alienated not only the *use*, but the *inheritance*, of power, they sunk, under the reign of the Caesars, into a vile and wretched populace, which must, in a few generations, have been totally extinguished, if it had not been continually recruited by the manumission of slaves and the influx of strangers.

❧ *Edward Gibbon*, The Decline and Fall of the Roman Empire, *1094–96, 1102*

Thomas Couture, *The Decadence of the Romans* (detail). MUSÉE D'ORSAY, PARIS, FRANCE.

Andre Durenceau, *Visigoths Pillage Rome.* NATIONAL GEOGRAPHIC SOCIETY.

FALL OF ROME

A.D. 455

THE Vandal King, Genseric, boldly advanced from the port of Ostia to the gates of the defenseless city. Rome and its inhabitants were delivered to the licentiousness of the Vandals and Moors, whose blind passions revenged the injuries of Carthage. The pillage lasted fourteen days and nights; and all that yet remained of public or private wealth, of sacred or profane treasure, was diligently transported to the vessels of Genseric.

It was difficult either to escape or to satisfy the avarice of a conqueror who possessed leisure to collect, and ships to transport, the wealth of the capital.

The haughty Vandal hoisted sail, and returned with a prosperous navigation to the port of Carthage. Many thousand Romans of both sexes, chosen for some useful or agreeable qualifications, reluctantly embarked on board the fleet of Genseric; and their distress was aggravated by the unfeeling barbarians, who, in the division of the booty, separated the wives from their husbands, and the children from their parents.

❧ *Edward Gibbon,* The Decline and Fall of the Roman Empire, *5–7*

DEFEATED ROME

A.D. 455

THE hill of the Capitol was formerly the head of the Roman empire, the citadel of the earth, the terror of kings; illustrated by the footsteps of so many triumphs, enriched with the spoils and tributes of so many nations. This spectacle of the world, how is it fallen! how changed! how defaced! The path of victory is obliterated by vines, and the benches of the senators are concealed by a dunghill.

Cast your eyes on the Palatine hill, and seek among the shapeless and enormous fragments the marble theatre, the obelisks, the colossal statues, the porticoes of Nero's palace: survey the other hills of the city, the vacant space is interrupted only by ruins and gardens. The forum of the Roman people, where they assembled to enact their laws and elect their magistrates, is now enclosed for the cultivation of pot-herbs, or thrown open for the reception of swine and buffaloes. The public and private edifices, that were founded for eternity, lie prostrate, naked, and broken, like the limbs of a mighty giant; and the ruin is the more visible, from the stupendous relics that have survived the injuries of time and fortune.

❧ *Edward Gibbon,* The Decline and Fall of the Roman Empire, *1438–39*

David Roberts, *The Forum, Rome.* MANCHESTER CITY ART GALLERIES, MANCHESTER, ENGLAND.

THE PRESENT

SOME OF THE NATIONS SEEN IN VISION BY THE PROPHET DANIEL*

A.D. 455–present

THIS image's . . . feet part of iron and part of clay.

And whereas thou sawest the feet and toes,
part of potters' clay, and part of iron,
the kingdom shall be divided; but there shall
be in it of the strength of the iron,
forasmuch as thou sawest the iron
mixed with miry clay. . . .

❦ *Daniel 2:32–33, 41*

Continued fulfillment of Nebuchadnezzar's dream as interpreted by Daniel (see page 92).

*The nations that King Nebuchadnezzar saw in his dreams in 597 B.C. are depicted on pages 204 through 209. Daniel's interpretation was realized by the fall of Rome in A.D. 455 and by the proliferation of many nations—and as iron would not cleave to miry clay, so neither would these nations cleave to one another.

FRANCE

Auguste Renoir, *Bal du Moulin de la Galette.* MUSÉE D'ORSAY, PARIS, FRANCE.

El Greco, *View of Toledo* (detail). H. O. HAVEMEYER COLLECTION,
BEQUEST OF MRS. H. O. HAVEMEYER, 1929 (29.100.6).
PHOTOGRAPH © 1992 THE METROPOLITAN MUSEUM OF ART, NEW YORK.

SPAIN

NATIONS SEEN BY THE PROPHET DANIEL

A.D. 455–present

AND as the toes of the feet were part of iron, and part of clay, so the kingdom shall be partly strong, and partly broken....

❧ *Daniel 2:42*

Continued fulfillment of Nebuchadnezzar's dream as interpreted by Daniel (see page 92).

TURKEY

Ivan Konstantinovich Aivazovsky, *View of Constantinople by Moonlight* (detail). MUSEUM OF THE REVOLUTION, ST. PETERSBURG, RUSSIA.

ITALY

Thomas Cole, *View of Florence, 1837.* © THE CLEVELAND MUSEUM OF ART, 1996. MR. AND MRS. WILLIAM H. MARLATT FUND, 1961.39.

ENGLAND

Giuseppe de Nittis, *Westminster.* PRIVATE COLLECTION.

Nations Seen by the Prophet Daniel

A.D. 455–present

AND whereas thou sawest iron mixed with miry clay,
they shall mingle themselves with the seed of men:
but they shall not cleave one to another,
even as iron is not mixed with clay.

❧ *Daniel 2:43*

Continued fulfillment of
Nebuchadnezzar's dream
as interpreted by Daniel
(see page 92).

RUSSIA   **Fyodor Alexeyev,** *Red Square, Moscow, 1801.* TRETYAKOV GALLERY, MOSCOW, RUSSIA.

POLAND

Bernardo Bellotto [Canaletto], *View of Warsaw from Praga.*
ROYAL CASTLE, WARSAW, POLAND.

Bernardo Bellotto [Canaletto], *Dresden from the Right Bank of the Elbe beneath the Augustus*
GERMANY *Bridge* (detail). STAATLICHE KUNSTSAMMLUNGEN DRESDEN, DRESDEN, GERMANY.

[209]

United States of America and the Gathering of Judah

A.D. 1948–present

Behold, thou shalt call a nation
that thou knowest not, and nations
that knew not thee shall run unto thee
because of the Lord thy God,
and for the Holy One of Israel;
for he hath glorified thee.

Thus saith the Lord God, Behold,
I will lift up mine hand to the Gentiles,
and set up my standard to the people:
and they shall bring thy sons in their arms,
and thy daughters shall be carried
upon their shoulders.

Lift up thine eyes round about, and see:
all they gather themselves together,
they come to thee: thy sons shall come
from far, and thy daughters
shall be nursed at thy side.

Then thou shalt see, and flow together,
and thine heart shall fear, and be enlarged;
because the abundance of the sea shall
be converted unto thee, the forces
of the Gentiles shall come unto thee.

Isaiah 55:5; 49:22; 60:4–5

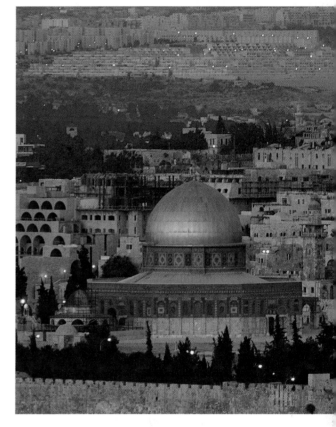

Dome of the Rock (detail). IRA BLOCK
PHOTOGRAPHY, NEW YORK.

The Statue of Liberty, New York Harbor.
HENRYK T. KAISER / UNIPHOTO, WASHINGTON, D.C.

The U.S. Capitol Building and the Washington Monument.
JUDY G. ROLFE / UNIPHOTO, WASHINGTON, D.C.

UNITED STATES
AIDS THE TRIBE
OF JUDAH

A.D. 1948–present

BUT ye shall be named
the Priests of the Lord:
men shall call you
the Ministers of our God:
ye shall eat the riches of the Gentiles,
and in their glory
shall ye boast yourselves.

And their seed shall be known
among the Gentiles, and their
offspring among the people:
all that see them shall acknowledge
them, that they are the seed
which the Lord hath blessed.

That ye may suck, and be satisfied
with the breasts of her consolations;
that ye may milk out, and be delighted
with the abundance of her glory.

For thus saith the Lord, Behold,
I will extend peace to her
like a river, and the glory of
the Gentiles like a flowing stream:
then shall ye suck, ye shall be borne
upon her sides, and be dandled
upon her knees.

Isaiah 61:6, 9; 66:11–12

James L. Stanfield. *The Wailing Wall, Jerusalem.* © NATIONAL GEOGRAPHIC SOCIETY.

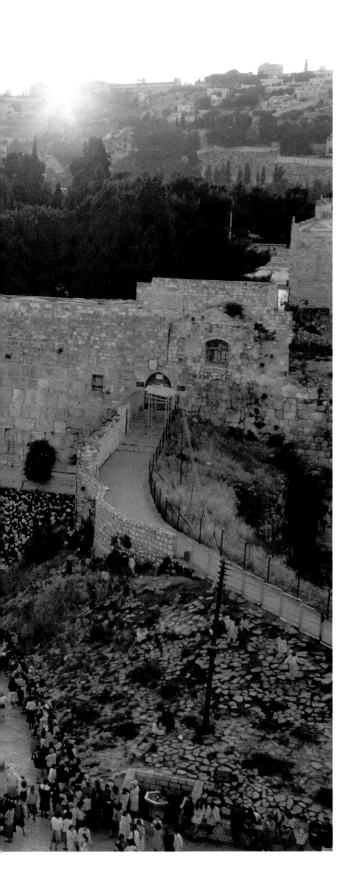

Gathering of the Tribe of Judah to Jerusalem

A.D. 1948–present

Thus saith the Lord;
I am returned unto Zion,
and will dwell in the midst
of Jerusalem: and Jerusalem
shall be called a city of truth;
and the mountain of the Lord of hosts
the holy mountain.

Thus saith the Lord of hosts;
Behold, I will save my people
from the east country,
and from the west country;

And I will bring them,
and they shall dwell
in the midst of Jerusalem:
and they shall be my people,
and I will be their God,
in truth and in righteousness.

So again have I thought in these days
to do well unto Jerusalem and
to the house of Judah: fear ye not.

Zechariah 8:3, 7–8, 15

**Return of Judah, dispersed by King
Nebuchadnezzar of Babylon in 586 B.C.
and by Titus of Rome in A.D. 70
(see pages 94–95 and 188–189).**

The Future

Honoré Daumier, *The Refugees.*
GERSTENBERT COLLECTION, BERLIN, GERMANY.

Return of the Ten Tribes taken captive by
King Shalmaneser of Assyria in 721 B.C.
(see pages 78–79).

Gathering of the Lost Ten Tribes

Future

Behold, I will bring them from the north
country, and gather them from the coasts
of the earth, and with them the blind
and the lame, the woman with child
and her that travaileth with child together:
a great company shall return thither.

They shall come with weeping,
and with supplications, will I lead them:
I will cause them to walk
by the rivers of waters in a straight way,
wherein they shall not stumble:
for I am a father to Israel,
and Ephraim is my firstborn.

And they shall be my people,
and I will be their God:

And I will give them one heart, and one way,
that they may fear me for ever, for the good
of them, and of their children after them.

Yea, I will rejoice over them to do them good,
and I will plant them in this land assuredly
with my whole heart and with my whole soul.

&ᴣ *Jeremiah 31:8–9; 32:38–39, 41*

RETURN OF THE LOST TEN TRIBES TO ISRAEL

Future

THEREFORE, behold, the days come,
saith the Lord, that it shall no more
be said, The Lord liveth, that
brought up the children of Israel
out of the land of Egypt;

But, The Lord liveth, that brought up
the children of Israel from the land
of the north, and from all the lands
whither he had driven them:
and I will bring them again into their
land that I gave unto their fathers.

For thus saith the Lord; Sing
with gladness for Jacob, and shout
among the chief of the nations:
publish ye, praise ye, and say,
O Lord, save thy people,
the remnant of Israel.

ঀ *Jeremiah 16:14–15; 31:7*

**Return of the Ten Tribes taken captive by
King Shalmaneser of Assyria in 721 B.C.
(see pages 78–79).**

David Roberts, *Sabaste, Ancient Samaria, April 17th, 1839* (plate 44 from Vol. 1 of
The Holy Land, engraved by Louis Haghe). STAPLETON COLLECTION, ENGLAND.

Frederic Edwin Church, *Jerusalem from the Mount of Olives.*
THE NELSON-ATKINS MUSEUM OF ART, KANSAS CITY, MISSOURI.
GIFT OF THE ENID AND CROSBY KEMPER FOUNDATION.

JERUSALEM—JUDAH AND ISRAEL SHALL BE ONE NATION

Future

AT that time they shall call Jerusalem
the throne of the Lord;
and all the nations shall be gathered
unto it, to the name of the Lord,
to Jerusalem: neither shall they walk
any more after the imagination
of their evil heart.

In those days the house of Judah
shall walk with the house of Israel,
and they shall come together
out of the land of the north
to the land that I have given for
an inheritance unto your fathers.

And I will make them
one nation in the land
upon the mountains of Israel;
and one king shall be king to them all:
and they shall be no more two nations,
neither shall they be divided into
two kingdoms any more at all.

❧ *Jeremiah 3:17–18;*
Ezekiel 37:22

GOSPEL PREACHED TO ALL THE WORLD

Future

Completed fulfillment of Nebuchadnezzar's dream as interpreted by Daniel (see page 92).

THOU sawest till that a stone was cut out without hands, which smote the image upon his feet that were of iron and clay, and brake them to pieces.

Then was the iron, the clay, the brass, the silver, and the gold, broken to pieces together, and became like the chaff of the summer threshingfloors; and the wind carried them away, that no place was found for them: and the stone that smote the image became a great mountain, and filled the whole earth.

And in the days of these kings shall the God of heaven set up a kingdom, which shall never be destroyed: and the kingdom shall not be left to other people, but it shall break in pieces and consume all these kingdoms, and it shall stand for ever.

❧ *Daniel 2:34–35, 44*

AND this gospel of the kingdom shall be preached in all the world for a witness unto all nations; and then shall the end come.

❧ *Matthew 24:14*

Stuart Paul Heimdal, *Stone Cut Out of Mountain.*
PRIVATE COLLECTION.

BATTLE OF ARMAGEDDON BEGINS

Future

FOR they are the spirits of devils, working miracles,
which go forth unto the kings of the earth
and of the whole world, to gather them
to the battle of that great day of God Almighty.

And he gathered them together
into a place called in the Hebrew tongue
Armageddon.

And there were voices, and thunders,
and lightnings; and there was a great earthquake,
such as was not since men were upon the earth,
so mighty an earthquake, and so great.

And the great city was divided into three parts,
and the cities of the nations fell:
and great Babylon came in remembrance
before God, to give unto her the cup
of the wine of the fierceness of his wrath.

For I will gather all nations against Jerusalem
to battle; and the city shall be taken,
and the houses rifled, and the women ravished;
and half of the city shall go forth into captivity,
and the residue of the people
shall not be cut off from the city.

❧ *Revelation 16:14, 16, 18–19;
Zechariah 14:2*

The Prophet Zechariah

Michelangelo Buonarroti.
THE SISTINE CHAPEL,
VATICAN PALACE, VATICAN.

Asher Brown Durand, *God's Judgment upon Gog.*
THE CHRYSLER MUSEUM OF ART, NORFOLK, VIRGINIA.
GIFT OF WALTER P. CHRYSLER, JR. (71.499).

Joseph Paul Pettit, *Armageddon, 1852.* YORK CITY ART
GALLERY, YORK, ENGLAND.

B A T T L E   O F   A R M A G E D D O N

Future

THEN shall the Lord go forth,
and fight against those nations,
as when he fought in the day of battle.

And men shall dwell in it, and there
shall be no more utter destruction;
but Jerusalem shall be safely inhabited.

And this shall be the plague
wherewith the Lord will smite all the people
that have fought against Jerusalem;
Their flesh shall consume away

while they stand upon their feet,
and their eyes shall consume away
in their holes, and their tongue
shall consume away in their mouth.

❧ *Zechariah 14:3, 11–12*

John Martin, *The Great Day of His Wrath.*
TATE GALLERY, LONDON, ENGLAND.

DESTRUCTION OF THE WICKED

Future

For, behold, the day cometh,
that shall burn as an oven;
and all the proud, yea,
and all that do wickedly,
shall be stubble: and the day
that cometh shall burn them up,
saith the Lord of hosts,
that it shall leave them neither
root nor branch.

Behold, the day of the Lord cometh,
cruel both with wrath and fierce anger,
to lay the land desolate: and he shall
destroy the sinners thereof out of it.

And I will punish the world
for their evil, and the wicked
for their iniquity; and I will cause
the arrogancy of the proud
to cease, and will lay low
the haughtiness of the terrible.

Therefore hath the curse
devoured the earth, and
they that dwell therein are desolate:
therefore the inhabitants of the earth
are burned, and few men left.

❧ *Malachi 4:1;*
Isaiah 13:9, 11; 24:6

END OF THE WORLD

Future

AND, lo, there was a great earthquake;
and the sun became black as sackcloth of hair,
and the moon became as blood;

And the stars of heaven fell unto the earth,
even as a fig tree casteth her untimely figs,
when she is shaken of a mighty wind.

And the heaven departed as a scroll
when it is rolled together; and every mountain
and island were moved out of their places.

And the kings of the earth, and the great men,
and the rich men, and the chief captains,
and the mighty men, and every bondman,
and every free man, hid themselves in the dens
and in the rocks of the mountains;

And said to the mountains and rocks,
Fall on us, and hide us from the face
of him that sitteth on the throne,
and from the wrath of the Lamb:

For the great day of his wrath is come;
and who shall be able to stand?

Revelation 6:12–17

Francis Danby, *The Opening of the Sixth Seal.*
NATIONAL GALLERY OF IRELAND, DUBLIN, IRELAND.

SECOND COMING
OF THE SAVIOR

Future

THE mountains quake at him,
and the hills melt, and the earth
is burned at his presence, yea,
the world, and all that dwell therein.

Who can stand before his indignation?
and who can abide in the fierceness of his anger?
his fury is poured out like fire,
and the rocks are thrown down by him.

Immediately after the tribulation
of those days shall the sun be darkened,
and the moon shall not give her light,
and the stars shall fall from heaven,
and the powers of the heavens shall be shaken:

And then shall appear the sign
of the Son of man in heaven:
and then shall all the tribes of the earth
mourn, and they shall see
the Son of man coming in the clouds
of heaven with power and great glory.

And he shall send his angels
with a great sound of a trumpet,
and they shall gather together
his elect from the four winds,
from one end of heaven to the other.

❧ *Nahum 1:5–6; Matthew 24:29–31*

Giovanni Battista Gaulli [Baciccio], *Triumph of the Name of Jesus* (detail). IL GESU, ROME, ITALY.

CHRIST IN GLORY

Future

For, behold, the Lord will come with fire, and
with his chariots like a whirlwind, to render his anger
with fury, and his rebuke with flames of fire.

For by fire and by his sword
will the Lord plead with all flesh:
and the slain of the Lord shall be many.

ꙮ *Isaiah 66:15–16*

I have trodden the winepress alone;
and of the people there was none with me:
for I will tread them in mine anger,
and trample them in my fury;
and their blood shall be sprinkled upon
my garments, and I will stain all my raiment.

For the day of vengeance is in mine heart,
and the year of my redeemed is come.

And I looked, and there was none to help;
and I wondered that there was none to uphold:
therefore mine own arm brought salvation
unto me; and my fury, it upheld me.

And I will tread down the people in mine anger,
and make them drunk in my fury, and
I will bring down their strength to the earth.

ꙮ *Isaiah 63:3–6*

Giuseppe Romei and Domenico Stagi, *Christ in Glory* (detail). s. maria del carmine church, florence, italy.

RESURRECTION

Future

THY dead men shall live, together
with my dead body shall they arise.
Awake and sing, ye that dwell in dust:
for thy dew is as the dew of herbs,
and the earth shall cast out the dead.

Marvel not at this:
for the hour is coming, in the
which all that are in the graves
shall hear his voice,

And shall come forth;
they that have done good,
unto the resurrection of life; and
they that have done evil, unto
the resurrection of damnation.

For the Lord himself shall descend
from heaven with a shout,
with the voice of the archangel,
and with the trump of God: and
the dead in Christ shall rise first:

Then we which are alive and remain
shall be caught up together
with them in the clouds, to meet
the Lord in the air: and so shall
we ever be with the Lord.

Isaiah 26:19; John 5:28–29;
1 Thessalonians 4:16–17

Frederic Leighton,
And the Sea Gave Up the Dead Which Were in It.
TATE GALLERY, LONDON, ENGLAND.

VICTORY OVER THE GRAVE

Future

AND have hope toward God,
which they themselves also allow,
that there shall be a resurrection
of the dead, both of the just and unjust.

Why should it be thought
a thing incredible with you,
that God should raise the dead?

Behold, I shew you a mystery;
We shall not all sleep,
but we shall all be changed,

In a moment, in the twinkling of an eye,
at the last trump: for the trumpet
shall sound, and the dead shall be raised
incorruptible, and we shall be changed.

For this corruptible must put on
incorruption, and this mortal
must put on immortality.

So when this corruptible shall have put
on incorruption, and this mortal shall
have put on immortality, then shall be
brought to pass the saying that is written,
Death is swallowed up in victory.

O death, where is thy sting?
O grave, where is thy victory?

Acts 24:15; 26:8; 1 Corinthians 15:51–55

Luca Signorelli, *Resurrection of the Dead.* DUOMO, ORVIETO, ITALY.

MILLENNIUM

Future

THERE shall be no more thence
an infant of days, nor an old man
that hath not filled his days:
for the child shall die an hundred years old;
but the sinner being an hundred years old
shall be accursed.

And they shall build houses,
and inhabit them;
and they shall plant vineyards,
and eat the fruit of them.

They shall not build, and another inhabit;
they shall not plant, and another eat:
for as the days of a tree
are the days of my people,
and mine elect shall long enjoy
the work of their hands.

They shall not labour in vain,
nor bring forth for trouble; for they
are the seed of the blessed of the Lord,
and their offspring with them.

And it shall come to pass,
that before they call, I will answer;
and while they are yet speaking,
I will hear.

❧ *Isaiah 65:20–24*

Claude Gellée [Claude Lorraine], *The Expulsion of Hagar* (detail). ALTE PINAKOTHEK MUSEUM, MUNICH, GERMANY.

CHRIST REIGNS
A THOUSAND YEARS
Future

THE wolf and the lamb
shall feed together, and the lion
shall eat straw like the bullock:
and dust shall be the serpent's meat.
They shall not hurt nor destroy in all
my holy mountain, saith the Lord.

And I saw thrones, and they sat upon
them, and judgment was given unto them:
and I saw the souls of them that
were beheaded for the witness of Jesus,
and for the word of God,
and which had not worshipped
the beast, neither his image,
neither had received his mark
upon their foreheads, or in their hands;
and they lived and reigned with Christ
a thousand years.

But the rest of the dead lived not again
until the thousand years were finished.
This is the first resurrection.

Blessed and holy is he that hath part
in the first resurrection: on such the
second death hath no power, but they shall
be priests of God and of Christ, and
shall reign with him a thousand years.

Isaiah 65:25; Revelation 20:4–6

Del Parson, *Behold Your Little Ones.*
PRIVATE COLLECTION.

Gathering for War at the End of the Millennium

Future

And I saw an angel come down from
heaven, having the key of the bottomless
pit and a great chain in his hand.

And he laid hold on the dragon,
that old serpent,
which is the Devil, and Satan,
and bound him a thousand years,

And cast him into the bottomless pit,
and shut him up, and set a seal
upon him, that he should deceive
the nations no more, till the thousand
years should be fulfilled: and after that
he must be loosed a little season.

And when the thousand years are expired,
Satan shall be loosed out of his prison,

And shall go out to deceive
the nations which are in the four quarters
of the earth, Gog and Magog,
to gather them together
to battle: the number of whom
is as the sand of the sea.

Revelation 20:1–3, 7–8

Stuart Paul Heimdal, *War at the End of the
Millennium.* PRIVATE COLLECTION.

WAR AT THE END OF THE MILLENNIUM

Future

AND they went up on
the breadth of the earth,
and compassed the camp
of the saints about,
and the beloved city:
and fire came down
from God out of heaven,
and devoured them.

And the devil
that deceived them
was cast into the lake
of fire and brimstone,
where the beast and
the false prophet are,
and shall be tormented
day and night
for ever and ever.

❧ *Revelation 20:9–10*

Peter Paul Rubens, *The Fall of
Phaeton.* © 1996 BOARD OF TRUSTEES,
NATIONAL GALLERY OF ART,
WASHINGTON, D.C.

THE LORD SHALL JUDGE THE WORLD

Future

LET the sea roar, and the fulness thereof;
the world, and they that dwell therein.

Let the floods clap their hands:
let the hills be joyful together

Before the Lord; for he cometh
to judge the earth: with righteousness
shall he judge the world,
and the people with equity.

For God shall bring every work into
judgment, with every secret thing,
whether it be good, or whether it be evil.

But why dost thou judge thy brother?
or why dost thou set at nought thy brother?
for we shall all stand before
the judgment seat of Christ.

For it is written, As I live, saith the Lord,
every knee shall bow to me,
and every tongue shall confess to God.

So then every one of us shall give
account of himself to God.

❧ *Psalm 98:7–9; Ecclesiastes 12:14;
Romans 14:10–12*

Michelangelo Buonarroti, *The Last Judgment* (detail).
THE SISTINE CHAPEL, VATICAN PALACE, VATICAN.

FINAL JUDGMENT

Future

AND I saw a great white throne,
and him that sat on it, from whose face
the earth and the heaven fled away;
and there was found no place for them.

And I saw the dead, small and great, stand
before God; and the books were opened:
and another book was opened, which is
the book of life: and the dead were judged
out of those things which were written
in the books, according to their works.

And the sea gave up the dead
which were in it; and death and hell
delivered up the dead which were in
them: and they were judged
every man according to their works.

But I say unto you, That every idle word
that men shall speak, they shall give
account thereof in the day of judgment.

For we must all appear
before the judgment seat of Christ;
that every one may receive the things
done in his body, according to that
he hath done, whether it be good or bad.

*Revelation 20:11–13; Matthew 12:36;
2 Corinthians 5:10*

Peter Paul Rubens, *The Large Last Judgment.* ALTE
PINAKOTHEK MUSEUM, MUNICH, GERMANY.

GLORY OF THE STARS

Future

THERE are also celestial bodies,
and bodies terrestrial:
but the glory of the celestial
is one, and the glory
of the terrestrial is another.

There is one glory of the sun,
and another glory of the moon,
and another glory of the stars:
for one star differeth
from another star in glory.

❧ *1 Corinthians 15:40–41*

While I was with
them in the world,
I kept them in thy name:
those that thou gavest me
I have kept,
and none of them is lost,
but the son of perdition.

❧ *John 17:12*

Thomas Cole, *The Voyage of Life: Youth.*

Glory of the Moon

Future

THERE are also celestial bodies,
and bodies terrestrial:
but the glory of the celestial
is one, and the glory
of the terrestrial is another.

There is one glory of the sun,
and another glory of the moon,
and another glory of the stars:
for one star differeth
from another star in glory.

❧ *1 Corinthians 15:40–41*

In my Father's house
are many mansions:
if it were not so,
I would have told you.
I go to prepare a place for you.

❧ *John 14:2*

Thomas Cole, Sketch for *The Cross and the World . . .*
The Pilgrim of the World on His Journey.
COLLECTION OF THE ALBANY INSTITUTE OF
HISTORY & ART, ALBANY, NEW YORK.

GLORY OF THE SUN

Future

THERE are also celestial bodies,
and bodies terrestrial:
but the glory of the celestial is one,
and the glory of the terrestrial
is another.

There is one glory of the sun,
and another glory of the moon,
and another glory of the stars:
for one star differeth
from another star in glory.

⁂ *1 Corinthians 15:40–41*

I knew a man in Christ
above fourteen years ago,
such an one caught up
to the third heaven.

⁂ *2 Corinthians 12:2*

And he shewed me a pure river
of water of life, clear as crystal,
proceeding out of the throne
of God and of the Lamb.

And there shall be no night there;
and they need no candle,
neither light of the sun;
for the Lord God giveth them light:
and they shall reign for ever and ever.

⁂ *Revelation 22:1, 5*

GLORY OF THE SUN

Andrea Sacchi, *La Divina Sapienza* (detail). PALAZZO BARBERINI.

THE WORLD IN ITS
FINAL CELESTIAL STATE

Future

AND I saw as it were a sea of glass
mingled with fire: and them that
had gotten the victory over the beast,
and over his image, and over his mark,
and over the number of his name, stand on
the sea of glass, having the harps of God.

The sun shall be no more thy light by day;
neither for brightness shall the moon give light
unto thee: but the Lord shall be unto thee
an everlasting light, and thy God thy glory.

Thy sun shall no more go down;
neither shall thy moon withdraw itself:
for the Lord shall be thine everlasting light,
and the days of thy mourning shall be ended.

Thy people also shall be all righteous:
they shall inherit the land for ever,
the branch of my planting, the work
of my hands, that I may be glorified.

And they that be wise shall shine
as the brightness of the firmament;
and they that turn many to righteousness
as the stars for ever and ever.

�֍ *Revelation 15:2;*
Isaiah 60:19–21; Daniel 12:3

Stuart Paul Heimdal, *Celestial World.*
PRIVATE COLLECTION.

BIBLIOGRAPHY

Durant, Will. *The Story of Civilization: Part I. Our Oriental Heritage.* New York: Simon and Schuster, 1954.

————. *The Story of Civilization: Part II. The Life of Greece.* New York: Simon and Schuster, 1939.

————. *The Story of Civilization: Part III. Caesar and Christ.* New York: Simon and Schuster, 1944.

Gibbon, Edward. *The Decline and Fall of the Roman Empire.* 1932 ed. Vol. II (A.D. 476–1461). New York: The Modern Library, 1932.

INDEX OF ARTISTS

INDEX OF ART AND ILLUSTRATIONS

Permissions

Artothek
16, 81, 184, 186, 218, 243, 253

Bridgeman Art Library, London/New York
110, 155

Bridgeman/Art Resource
22, 49, 64, 66, 83, 137, 147, 164, 221

Cameraphoto/Art Resource
207

Erich Lessing/Art Resource
10, 27, 59, 78, 121, 125, 167, 188, 190, 205

Giraudon/Art Resource
74, 151, 160, 197

Jewish Museum/Art Resource
39, 51, 94

Kavaler/Art Resource
32

Nimatallah/Art Resource
178

Scala/Art Resource
6, 9, 18, 24, 123, 149, 156, 162, 172, 173, 174, 180, 208, 234, 236, 240

Superstock
22

Tate Gallery/Art Resource
137, 230, 239

Victoria & Albert Museum/Art Resource
71, 73, 85, 183, 184

Werner Forman/Art Resource
49